"...a funny and honest look at jobs that are overpaid, over respected and generally require little work for a lot of perks."
—Associated Press

"Bing is always funny, but this time, he has really outdone himself. And that's no bull."
—*Houston Chronicle*

"Like *The Office*'s wisecracking David Brent, Mr. Bing doggy-paddles in the choppy waters between straight-laced corporate expertise and slapstick satire."
—*New York Observer*

"...a tongue-in-cheek look at some of those head-scratching positions your lazy friends make money in and that make you consider giving your two weeks' notice ... till you realize your job is just as bullshit as theirs."
—Playboy

"Fans of Bing will hardly be surprised that he again proves himself a shrewd observer of society and commentator on corporate life."
—*BusinessWeek*

Collins
An Imprint of HarperCollinsPublishers

100 Bullshit Jobs

... And How to Get Them

Stanley Bing

A hardcover edition of this book was published in 2006 by Collins.

HarperCollins books may be purchased for educational, business, or sales promotional use. For information, please write to: Special Markets Department, HarperCollins Publishers, 10 East 53rd Street, New York, New York 10022.

FIRST COLLINS PAPERBACK PUBLISHED 2007.

Library of Congress Cataloging-in-Publication is available upon request.

978-0-06-073480-0

06 07 08 09 10 ❖/RRD 10 9 8 7 6 5 4 3 2 1

Dedication

To my dad, a college professor and a very learned man, who carried in his wallet a business card that he would present only to those who offered theirs. In the middle of the card was his name in fine, raised type. And underneath, where the personal information should have been, was the simple statement:

"**I'm something of a bullshit artist myself.**"

Acknowledgments

I'd like to thank George Orwell, whose real name was Eric Blair and who worked for the totalitarian organization known as the British Broadcasting Corporation, for recognizing that in the future only bullshit will be accepted as truth.

I'd like to thank all the people I knew when I was in show business for teaching me how to shine people on as an alternative to giving them bad news.

I'd like to thank Colin Powell, perhaps the only truly ambivalent man in a cadre of true believers, for shucking off his inconvenient coat of doubt, going to the United Nations, and selling that puppy.

I'd like to thank my editor, David Hirshey, who has forgotten more about bullshitting than most people ever know.

And most of all, I'd like to thank you, my readers, for buying this book. You make it all worthwhile. You're beautiful.

All paid jobs absorb and degrade the mind.

—ARISTOTLE

Contents

100 Bullshit Jobs...and How to Get Them

100 Bullshit Jobs

... And How to Get Them

Serious Introductory Bullshit

Not long ago, a friend of mine who occupies a very high position in a mind-bogglingly enormous conglomerate called his boss, a veritable titan of industry, to inform him of a developing situation.

"Bob," said my friend, whose name is also Bob, "I'm going to acquire that $15 billion operation in China I was telling you about when we flew together last Thursday."

There was a profound silence on the other end of the phone. My friend Bob held his breath. This was an important strategic priority for him, a very big bite of a potentially disastrous apple. When he had broached the subject on the corporate jet heading down to Dallas, the chairman had seemed preoccupied, unfocused, had looked out the window the whole time, and then reverted to cursory golf chat. Now presented with the reality of this awesome financial and operational step, what would big Bob, the steward of the entire enterprise, known for his sharp mind, caustic wit, hot temper, cold heart, and unpredictable emotional infrastructure, do to little Bob?

"Bob," said the chairman thoughtfully after a time, "have you ever been to Paris?"

My friend's mind whirled. What could this possibly be about? Was there a hidden agenda here that was going to pop up and bite him in the butt? "Sure, Bob," he said carefully. And waited.

"When you're there," said the chairman, "what hotel do you stay at? I used to invariably go to the Crillon, but I'm getting tired of that. I think the scene may be more interesting elsewhere. I don't want to cross the river, so keep me on the Right Bank, but what would you suggest?"

"Well," said my friend, "I like the Ritz a lot."

"Thanks," said the chairman warmly, and, after a short disquisition on the wonders of the south of France in spring, rang off.

Bob did the acquisition without further consultation, except for a presentation to his board, of course, which also seemed distracted while he was laying out the plan, and then, after approving it, had lunch.

Is this a story of corporate malfeasance? Of responsibility shirked and the shareholders' interests once again trampled in the hot dust of executive laziness, inattentiveness, and stupidity? No, it isn't, because my friend Bob knows what he is doing and will make everybody a lot of money in China. So it's not about that. What it is, however, is a stunning and pungent demonstration of bullshit in action.

Bob's chairman has a bullshit job. He knows it. He revels in it. And in this tale, we see him at the top of his bullshit game, performing his stunningly bullshit function with ease and distinction. The board, which should come as no surprise, is a bullshit institution and conforms to all expectations in that regard, including the part about lunch. Throughout, the bullshit artists are able to operate in a pleasant, no-stress, friendly environment provided by guys like my friend Bob, those willing to assume the actual mantle of hard work and all the unpleasantness that comes with it.

Opportunities in the lush brown field of bullshit employment are virtually limitless. My publisher told me to limit this exercise to 100 jobs for some kind of bullshit marketing consideration, but I can tell you that I could have doubled that number easily, and that's focusing only on the domestic front and California. The global possibilities are equally limitless, especially in France, where fully 46 percent of all people are engaged in some kind of bullshit occupation, and Japan, where they hire people to help you get on and off escalators.

What do all these people have in common? They all have bullshit jobs. And guess what? They're having fun, making a living, and enjoying their lives, perhaps more than you are right now as you wolf down that tuna sandwich before you push your nose back on that grindstone.

Ah, bullshit jobs! God must have loved them, since he made so many of them. Actually, Abraham Lincoln said that about something completely different—the common man, I think, which is why they put his head on the penny. Anyhow, the people lucky and skillful enough to have secured bullshit employment are everywhere, in virtually every field from ayurvedic healing to yoga franchising—I couldn't come up with a z. The folks who work in these coveted bullshit positions enjoy the best lives imaginable—they are paid well, they work very little, and their professions are highly respected because nobody really knows what they do.

What, for instance, are the actual functions performed by a McKinsey consultant? Other than sitting around making people nervous? None. That's what he does. And by next Tuesday, he'll probably be your boss's boss! You think I'm kidding? Read the paper. About half a mile from me is another division of my corporation. Not long ago, they named one of their McKinsey consultants to the No. 2 position at the headquarters operation. The encouraging wrinkle here is that instead of the usual story of the consultant snuffing out a real, live, nonbullshit working executive, the McKinsey guy is superseding another McKinsey guy! Who says there are no happy endings in business?

What does an aromatherapist actually do? Sniff things? Yes! For big, fragrant bucks, that's what!

When the executive vice president of new media gives you his card, what is he offering? Who knows? Vaporware! For six figures plus a bonus equal to 100 percent of his base salary, in reward for the quality and size of the digital bullshit he's capable of marketing.

What is a shrink actually doing when he or she is nodding at a suffering depressive? Nodding, we know that much. Beyond that? Essentially unknown. I know PhDs who make upward of $300 an hour for that. On the other hand, my shrink is worth every penny. Is that because what he practices is not bullshit? Or that his bullshit is simply better than any other, at least for me? Who knows?

This book begins with certain assumptions:

1. A fair amount of bullshit in anybody's job is, a priori, a good thing, however you define bullshit, which is an interesting subject in itself that we will pursue in a moment.

2. The ability to bullshit is what separates happy beasts from miserable mankind.

3. There are costs for obtaining and maintaining a job that is fundamentally bullshit, but all good things come at a price.

4. All jobs, no matter how apparently full of content, can be rendered into a high-octane, lucrative, completely insubstantial charade over time.

5. There are some people who have a negative take on bullshit jobs. If you've read this far, you're probably not one of them.

To begin, we must ask some critical questions that, although they are about bullshit, are not of it, because bullshit is in itself a serious subject and worthy of discourse that is not completely full of it.

I'm not sure what the other questions are, but I know what the first one ought to be.

A Critical Question

What is bullshit?

Is it, as suggested by Harry G. Frankfurt, the author of a rather censorious but best-selling bullshit book on the subject, the product of moral morons who are content to live in the gray zone where there is no truth and no untruth, that the bullshitter cares less about the truth than the liar? This seems rather severe to me, even if true, or not true. In fact, I don't care if it's true or not, come to think of it.

Is it silly stuff, like you see in all the Web sites dedicated to bullshit on the Internet? Now we're a little closer but still not quite there. Some bullshit is silly, true, but just because something is idiotic doesn't make it bullshit. Some very smart things are completely full of it. Have you read any string theory?

Is it, as Penn & Teller demonstrate in their truculent and amusing cable program, all the hypocritical garbage that clogs our social system? The faith healers, astrologers, dowsers, marketers? Yes, but to define a thing by its most egregious and worst examples is unfair, I think. There is bad bullshit, just as there is bad art of all kinds. But there is also good art. And that, my friends, is perhaps the most precious commodity that humanity can produce!

Ultimately what we are looking for here is a definition of bullshit that is not bullshit. This turns out to be difficult, so I'm not even going to attempt it. Why bust my hump when I can be true to the spirit of this exercise and not turn a bullshit assignment into something rigorous?

Just a few salient thoughts, though, might be in order, because even though a job may be a bullshit job, that doesn't mean it isn't a job at all, with bullshit duties that must be performed with energy, if not seriousness. So:

A Few Salient Thoughts

- Bullshit is not what is true, but what we wish might be true. That is, bullshit is hope.

• Bullshit is what you say when you have nothing to say. It is the effort to fill the void between knowledge and ignorance. And it takes the kind of finesse, practice, and talent that characterizes the pursuit of other creative human activities, which is why we call its practitioners artists.

• Bullshit is what passes for the truth until the real thing comes along. For instance, when a man is losing his hair, he will very often spend time fluffing up what he has left in the mirror. He bullshits himself into thinking he looks better until he can see his scalp gleaming in the unkind glare of the bathroom light. When that happens, he may very well shave his head completely and then bullshit himself into believing he looks better that way than he did with hair. In this we also see that the first consumer of an individual's bullshit is, and must be, him- or herself.

• The truth hurts, but bullshit is kind. Lies are corrosive, but bullshit is a warm puppy.

• Bullshit is not a hobby; it's a way of life. It is a strategy, a game, a jolly thumb in the eye of anything that is not bullshit. Bullshit is fun.

• The job that embodies all these characteristics will be (1) easy, (2) prestigious, (3) pay well, and (4) offer a path to even bigger bullshit jobs.

All of this sounds pretty attractive, doesn't it? Of course, it's not for everybody. There are quite a few who look down their nose at bullshit and the artists who tender it.

These are generally serious, tedious people who don't realize that they, too, are bullshitting somebody about something. If you're one of them, go away right now. Better yet, buy this book for a friend who knows what to do with it.

The problem, however, for even the most ambitious bullshit artist, is how to differentiate "real" jobs from bullshit ones.

As a public service, then, I'll take a cursory stab at how one might view this issue, and put it into a table that you can read easily, since we've had a lot of uninterrupted text and you must be getting kind of tired by now.

Not Bullshit	Bullshit
The miracle of childbirth	The NFL halftime show
Massive heart attack at the age of 50	Receding hairline at the age of 50
Receding hairline at the age of 30	Massive heart attack while having sex
Divorce	Divorce lawyers
Art	Art criticism
God	Religious zealots
Religious zealots with weapons	Plastic silverware in first class
Anderson Cooper	George Stephanopoulos
Health	Healers
War	Warmongers
Truth	Cheez Whiz

Now, I could make an attempt to elucidate all the things that unite the stuff in column two and distinguish that matter from the items in column one, but I think it would be a waste of time. That said, there are certain things we could chew the fat about for a minute on the subject. All the items on the left side of our table exercise a certain muscle in the human soul. The items on the right have to spend a lot of time marketing, pitching, explaining themselves.

Finally, I suppose, it comes down to this: the stuff on the left is fragile, precious, and easily broken. God, for instance. How hard we have to work to reach Him! Just as we feel we're getting close, He or She slips from us, either because He is busy elsewhere or because we are. Or Anderson Cooper? For a few moments now, he has embodied something new, honest, and unpredictable in the sodden state of journalism. But for how long? How long will it take for him to descend into self-parody?

The stuff on the right? It's durable. Predictable. Easy to access and replicate. It will never go away. It will always be with us. And in this book, we will learn how each of us can construct a successful, happy, fulfilling life built on a pile of it.

A Short Course in Bullshitting

Artists are people who use techniques that they have mastered to work intuitively, to reach down into their own soul and into the souls of others to find a mutual truth they can sell for money, unless they're Van Gogh, who didn't live to see his work ever purchased by anybody. That is a complete tragedy that I hope to help you avoid.

Let's start with some critical choices.

Step One: *Choose your medium.* Some work in oils. Some work in words. Some really terrific bullshit artists work in video, especially those who produce totally boring loops that you see in museums dedicated to the moving image. Your medium may be memos or lunch conversation or e-mails or phone calls or text messages—there are as many ways of conveying bullshit as there are new media making outrageous claims for themselves in *The Wall Street Journal*. But a conscious choice of the way you transmit your art is all-important. The way you work in paper will not be the same as the way you work in vodka.

Step Two: *Choose your technique.* You may mix a little truth, a touch of prevarication, a whit of humor, a tablespoon of ire. Great bullshit is as varied and multihued as the gorgeous tapestry of human experience. Many great business executives' bullshit takes the form of rage. Parents often choose to work in a subtle mixture of guilt and love, and garage mechanics, always seeking to put off for tomorrow what they might do today, wield a potent blend of promises, excuses, and hope. This is art! Feel it with your gut!

Step Three: *Choose your time.* Yes, as Ecclesiastes said, to everything there is a season. First, there is a time for pure, unvarnished truth. I don't know why the truth always has to be unvarnished, but that seems to be the case. I've had many nice pieces of furniture that were varnished, and they were far more beautiful and useful than the cruddy unvarnished ones, but I guess that's beside the point. The truth is preferable to a lie. On the other hand, lies, too, have their place. People who can't use mendacity in the service of their agendas are at a significant disadvantage. At the same time, there are many occasions when lies are not only unnecessary, they are, in fact, inadvisable. So—between bald truth and naked lies, lies the land in which bullshit is highly necessary, functional, and appreciated. The ability to offer it with skill, tact, and impunity can be understood as the triumph of maturity and civilization over the forces of barbarism, darkness, and impotence. So choose your time, choose it well, and have no fear or compunction. You are, in a sense, doing the work of all artists—shaping reality to the needs of society and, of course, yourself.

Step Four: *Stick to the knitting.* Artists suffer from a bad professional hazard: they tend toward flights of fancy. Keep in mind, you are in this thing day in, day out, year after year, and the key to longevity in any business is getting the mandatory duties of your bullshit job done. Bullshitting is not the same as excuse making. You need to do the job, whatever it is. And in every job, there is a portion that is *not* bullshit.

This is an important concept for you, so I'm going to say it again. In every job, there is a portion that is not bullshit. In the work of a funeral director, for example, there is the part where you have to pump embalming fluid into the corpse, prepare it for viewing by people who used to love the deceased, and minister to those who are seriously unhappy. All of that is most certainly devoid of bullshit. The part where you convince the family to spend $7,500 on a solid oak casket ringed in gold filigree? Now, that's when your art kicks in.

Before you come a long line of illustrious bullshit artists of the past and present who guide all who have read this far. They include figures from the mythological (and even biblical) to the all-too-real titans who have shaped our world and continue to do so.

Great Bullshitters of the Past and Present

THE SNAKE, GARDEN OF EDEN	Undercommunicated the effects of strategic advice offered to unsuspecting clients.
DAVID, KING OF ISRAEL	Extremely good poet and statesman, but sent Uriah, the husband of the woman he loved, Bathsheba, out to die in battle. That's really bullshit. I hate it when senior officers do that. I had a chairman once who sent his girlfriend's husband, who was also a vice president of the corporation, to Rio for two years, and then proceeded to buy the wife, who was his vice president of operations, a new Porsche. They used to show up at retreats in matching velvet jumpsuits! Come on!
AUTHOR OF *BEOWULF*	Whipped up an excellent beginning, ran out of steam, padded poem outrageously with extremely tedious bullshit after that.

MARCUS CRASSUS	Greedy guy, made tons of money in old Rome by investing in real estate at a very low price, then "waiting for a fire," and afterward rebuilding and selling condos for big bucks. When fire didn't arrive on schedule, was famous for starting them. When he died, the Parthians poured molten gold into his mouth and then decapitated him. What a waste of gold!
HENRY VIII	Created an entire new religion, persecuting the old one, simply because he didn't like divorce laws under existing theological infrastructure. Hey, nobody likes divorce laws (particularly in New York State), but we don't go around killing all the divorce lawyers, now, do we? I mean, could we?
MARIE ANTOINETTE	Her "let them eat cake" will live as one of the great bullshit jokes of the eighteenth century. Of course, she got pretty badly punished for it.

ROBESPIERRE	Fed a raft of bullshit about freedom and the rights of man to the people of France, then went on to kill everybody who pissed him off. The killing is not the bullshit part. But let's leave out the philosophical underpinning, okay?
NEVILLE CHAMBERLAIN	Declared "peace in our time" while selling out Czechoslovakia to Hitler.
JUDITH MILLER	Marketed whole weapons of mass destruction thing to readers of *The New York Times* while cozying up to bullshit sources.
JAMES FREY	Lied to Oprah.

Calculating ß: The Bullshit Quotient of Your Job

Like I said, the understanding that many apparently 100-percent bullshit occupations have some percentage of actual content is key to your evaluation and appreciation of the jobs that lie ahead for you. I'd like to take a moment, then, to investigate a brief means of scientifically calculating the actual bullshit component of any occupation, to help you make your ultimate selection.

The fundament of all that guides the physical universe may be expressed in one simple equation first formulated by Isaac Newton, and this guy didn't have an ounce of bullshit in him. Here is the formula:

F = MA

Or

Force equals Mass multiplied by Acceleration

That is, the force of something is a function of how heavy it is and how fast it is picking up speed.

Stay with me here. It will be worth it. This equation is not only the basis of the laws of physical motion. In another, better-known form—$E=mc^2$—it is the core of Einstein's theory of relativity, a body of work that looks very much like bullshit but really isn't, at least for those who have seen a mushroom cloud or used to live around Chernobyl.

First, let's think about the three elements involved in Newton's original equation:

- Force: or to put it another way, power. Economic power. Management power. Sexual power. The secret of life.

- Mass: or to put it another way, weight. As in, I put on weight. He's a lightweight. He ain't heavy, he's my brother.

- Acceleration: or to put it another way, speed. If there's anything we like almost as much as power, it's speed. Fast car. Fast food. Can't talk. Gotta run.

Your power is equal to how heavy you are, boosted by how much faster you are going than you were five minutes ago.

- Okay, then: β ισ τηε ποωερ . . . oh, sorry. β is the power of the bullshit in any of the jobs we'll be looking at in this book.

• Mass—what makes things heavy? In looking at jobs, that would have to be the hours one is forced to put in (H); the amount of times one is likely to be abused by one's management or clients, on a scale of 10 (A); the value of the package of perks associated with the employment, in thousands, with a minimum number of 1 (P); and finally and not the least important, the salary ($), in tens of thousands. The higher the number of hours, the more it will reduce the quotient of the job—since great bullshit jobs require very little presence, I think. We can therefore express the mass of the job as follows:

$$\textbf{Mass} = \frac{\textbf{Abuse} \times \textbf{Perks} \times \textbf{\$alary}}{\textbf{Hours}}$$

$$\textbf{Or}\ldots\ \textbf{M} = \frac{\textbf{AP\$}}{\textbf{H}}$$

• Acceleration, likewise, is a rather simple function—how fast is your career growing over time? This may be expressed as G, or a number between 1 and 10. How does it work? Well, if you're a personal publicist who had eight big clients last year, and this year you just had Brad Pitt? You're doing great, baby! Give yourself a G of 8, because one Brad Pitt adds up to at least eight schmendricks!

Our final equation, then, looks like this:

$$\beta = \frac{\mathbf{AP\$}}{\mathbf{H}}\,\mathbf{(G)}$$

And here's how it works, looking at an average corporate bullshit job like mine:

$$\beta = \frac{\text{Abuse} \times \textbf{25 thousand worth of perks} \times \textbf{12 in tens of thousands}}{\textbf{35 hours (golf not included)}}\,\mathbf{(3)}$$

. . . assuming that the job is growing at a rate of 3, which is moderate and slightly optimistic for most of us.

This scientific calculation gives us a ß of exactly 128.57, a number over 100, which makes it a truly bullshit job indeed, so congratulations, whoever you are, you're doing great, and so am I.

100 Bullshit Jobs

...And How to Get Them

1

Advertising Executive

Create perceived need/value for inherently generic or worthless products

> Many a small thing has been made large by the right kind of advertising.
>
> **Mark Twain**

$$: Ground-level workers with writing ability move quickly to the top, immediately snagging low to mid-six figures; those who can spin mythological concepts surrounding quotidian household objects can command up to seven figures.

ß: 100. It's easy to sell bullshit to people who are in the market for it, but when they're not buying your bullshit, life is not worth living.

Skills Required: The ability to apply great attributes, moving story lines, heroic character traits, humor, and passion.

Helpful capabilities include: experience in ensemble acting, improvisational theater, sales, public relations, graphic design, and team sports.

Duties: Depends on what portion of the alimentary canal you occupy—the top where the mouth is located or the other end.

Generally, the advertising campaign begins with a conversation with the client, who believes his product or service will be helped by spending inordinate amounts of money for the branding and high-concept positioning a great ad campaign provides. Once you have the mandate to do what is necessary from him a variety of things happen. Managers manage. Writers write. Graphic guys do their visual magic. Researchers lob in market analysis. Sometimes the group gets together and brainstorms, whipping up a froth of bullshit that lifts the entire boat. At last a campaign comes together and you go back in and pitch the client in a pithy, snazzy, riveting dog-and-pony presentation that leaves everybody gasping and nails the cat to the wall.

> We grew up founding our dreams on the infinite promise of American advertising. I still believe that one can learn to play the piano by mail and that mud will give you a perfect complexion.
>
> **Zelda Fitzgerald**

Famous Examples: J. Walter Thompson, who in some ways began the entire business in the nineteenth century with the first print campaigns. Why should a cracker have any name except "cracker"? Thompson saw that it could, and there followed Ritz, Saltines, Uneeda

Biscuits—get it? You need a biscuit! Ha! About twenty years ago, J. Walter Thompson was acquired by Martin Sorrell, one of the great business bullshitters of all time and the master of the bloody, Pyrrhic, unfriendly takeover. What a guy. I was at a meeting with Sir Martin once in which he addressed a bunch of some two hundred senior business executives with a mélange of wisdom, insight, and self-important claptrap. My favorite moment was when he received a question from the audience about the efficacy of hostile acquisitions. He took a moment, looked deep into his vast wad of personal experience, and said, "I don't believe there is such a thing." Now, that, my friends, is world-class bullshit, and it's not a coincidence that Sorrell is in the advertising business, whose mission it is to dream it up, flambé it, and present it on a platter to the people of the world.

How to Get It: Pitching is at the heart of this particular bullshit game. If you've got a gift for shameless presentation of the ersatz, watch a lot of TV—preferably stoned now and then. Study hard on how stuff is sold to mass and niche audiences and how a worthless bolus of gunk can be turned into a child's toy. Then go to New York. Madison Avenue is one block east of Fifth.

The Upside: Great expense account living, see your handiwork everywhere, the wonderful feeling of being creative and corporate at the same time.

The Downside: Must take meetings with the AFLAC duck.

The Dark Side: You're considered a dinosaur at forty.

Where You Go from Here: Politics—as an advisor to human products.

2

Agent

Talk on phone, take percentage

> Let every eye negotiate for itself and trust no agent.
>
> **Shakespeare**

$$: Seven figures is not out of the ordinary, and the lunch action is astounding.

ß: 54–172.

Skills Required: Shine people on or cut them dead, depending on the situation. One must possess a serious love of bullshit in all its many forms.

Duties: Make sure that no client of yours ever takes it up the butt.

Famous Examples: Swifty Lazar, who will be remembered for his Oscar parties; Norman Brokaw and Lou Weiss of the William Morris Agency, who I believe knew Jolson; Binky Urban, whose name comes up more often in New York book chat than Proust's or Jerry McGuire.

> I'm not currently represented. I'm with the William Morris Agency.
>
> **Larry Gelbart, to Johnny Carson**

How to Get It: To become a successful agent, all you need to do is get a foot in the door at the very lowest level and then show yourself to be a meat-eating barracuda from the get-go. A lot of agents, although not as many as in the past, come in through the mailroom. Others start as assistants and very quickly begin to take on unknown and marginal petitioners, one of whose success will immediately reap huge career gains. You don't have to be all that educated, either. Just smart. Or not. There are certainly a lot of stupid agents.

The Upside: Lots of people groveling as you eat your gravlax. A sense of achievement in the success of others, as long as you're getting a piece of it.

The Downside: People sucking on your face all day. And there comes a time when Steve doesn't seat you at the right table.

The Dark Side: You die alone and unmourned.

Where You Go from Here: Upward and upward into the stratosphere of the profession, where the lines blur between superagent and producer and lawyer.

Allergist

Inject placebos to offset hypochondria in children

$$: Low to mid-six figures, if you're serious about it.

ß: 81.4.

Skills Required: Know how to give scratch tests and small injections, also treat the occasional wheezing attack.

Duties: Give shots, go "hmmm" when confronted with welt or rash. Keep up on the relevant pharmacology. A certain amount of golfing is usually required.

Famous Example: Your area's most successful allergist.

How to Get It: Here's the big hurdle—you will have to go to medical school and earn an MD, most decidedly a low-bullshit endeavor. There's blood and sputum and really sick people. After that, you're pretty much home free.

The Upside: Not a whole lot of death.

The Downside: Crushing boredom.

The Dark Side: Your application for membership to Pebble Beach is rejected.

Where You Go from Here: Proctology school.

Q: I'm a thirty-year-old woman. Recently I have started having a terrible experience. When I am having sex, in the moment of my orgasm, my throat closes and I cannot breathe for a long time. Last time was scary because I spent more than 30 minutes with my throat completely closed and every 1 or 2 minutes I could take a big breath and again it closed. I felt like I was going to die; my partner gave me mouth-to-mouth respiration and I survived. I am really scared about having an orgasm again.

A: Some people do have asthma attacks during or after strenuous activity. This can sometimes be treated by using an inhaler prior to engaging in the activity.

Columbia University health web site

4

Anything Emeritus

Live on laurels

> I don't want to be emeritus anything.
>
> **Don Hewitt, founder, former executive producer, *60 Minutes***

$$: Not what it used to be, but still, not bad for doing nothing.

ß: 102.

Skills Required: Stay vertical for at least three hours a day.

Duties: Show up. Or not.

Famous Examples: Walter Cronkite, Jimmy Carter, Bill Cosby, who has between 100 and 120 honorary degrees.

How to Get It: Kick ass for forty years and then sit back and wait for people to offer you a no-work position for respectable compensation.

The Upside: License for laziness.

The Downside: What your mouth tastes like when you wake up from a five-hour nap.

The Dark Side: Forget what you had for breakfast, and then, after a while, forget whether you had breakfast.

Where You Go from Here: Fairlawn.

5

Aquarium Cleaner for the Rich

Dredge fish feces out of tanks nicer than most people's apartments

$$: $35,000–$85,000.

> No one can feel as helpless as the owner of a sick goldfish.
>
> **Kin Hubbard**

ß: 27–68. (Jobs that deal in actual excreta ironically may involve a lot less bullshit than you might think.)

Skills Required: Good with squeegee, don't hit the fish with the net, don't drip on the floor, ability to schmooze endlessly about fish.

Duties: Maintain exquisitely delicate ecosystems that are intimately linked to the emotional infrastructure of powerful, infantile, excessively affluent capitalists.

Famous Example: Scott McClellan.

How to Get It: Find a job at a pet store, meet patrons obsessed with pH and salinity of water, learn which genus and species of fish play best with others.

You may also choose to become a midlevel corporate executive working for a mogul, end up cleaning the fish tank, and never reach the point where you are comfortable enough with your station to delegate that job. After six corporate reorganizations and two divestitures, the fish tank gig is all that is left of your former role as executive vice president of development, so you just keep on doing that. Hey, algae is not the only substance that is green.

The Upside: Join Aquarist Paradise, which describes itself as "a global community of aquarists that share a common bond: our passion for fishkeeping . . . and our desire to share our knowledge/experiences with like-minded aquarists."

The Downside: Fish mung.

The Dark Side: Fish die horrible deaths with great regularity, often eaten by their associates.

Where You Go from Here: Red Lobster.

6

Aromatherapist

Use smelly things to make people feel better

$$: $25,000 for simple scalp workers to $87,500 for those with full-body expertise.

ß: 73.8—not the aroma part, the therapy part.

Skills Required: Good sense of smell and ability to not retch at continuous odor of patchouli and musk.

> Aromatherapy is essentially an interaction between the therapist, client, and essential oils, working together to bring forth the healing energy which will help the client regain their sense of well being and vitality.
>
> **Jade Shutes**

Duties: Mix potions and unguents and rub on bodies, including:

Cananga odorata; Chamaemelum nobile; Citrus limon; Citrus sinensis; Eucalyptus globulus; Lavandula angustifolia; Melaleuca alternifolia; Pelargonium graveolens; Rosa damascena; Rosmarinus officinalis; Salvia sclarea; and many more.

I'm not sure which of the goos the aromatherapist I visited a few years ago used on my head. She took off my shirt. I lay down with my face in a little doughnut of leather and soft foam rubber. She washed my hair with some stuff that smelled very good. And then she rubbed my scalp for about an hour, which produced a variety of physical sensations in various other parts of my body. When I left, any anxiety I had felt before entering was pretty much gone and I was about $400 lighter, having also purchased a bunch of hair products in the hopes that self-aromatizing would produce a similar result. In perhaps a tribute to the efficacy of the profession, it did not.

Famous Example: René-Maurice Gattefosse, who invented the art and science of aromatherapy in 1928. He discovered that people with emotional and physical ailments responded to being slavered with various smelly oils by a person purporting to be a practitioner of a science of some sort.

How to Get It: The National Association for Holistic Aromatherapy suggests a thirty-hour minimum to establish the foundations. This includes a focus on ancient cultures, insights into up to twenty essential oils, their production and use, an understanding of absorption and the systems—lymphatic, limbic, immune—that the oils are intended to work on both emotionally and physically. You must pass an examination offered by a licensed aromatherapy school. So roll up your sleeves and keep your nose clean.

The Upside: Your bullshit doesn't stink.

The Downside: You must smear a variety of substances on people who smell funny to begin with.

The Dark Side: Engorged nose syndrome leads to gigantic beezer.

Where You Go from Here: Salad dresser.

7

Ayurvedic Healer

Ayurveda is an ancient science based upon effecting a balance between body, mind, and spirit to reduce susceptibility to disease in ailing ex-hippies

$$: Not important. If you're into money, become another kind of healer. Ayurveda is based on the Vedas, the Hindu scriptures that are thousands and thousands of years old. You need to be spiritual, not mercenary. That said, a person has to eat, so try to charge at least $100 per hour, or 33 percent of the going rate for MD psychiatrists in suburban communities where people don't have enough to think about. The really big money comes from

> The most commonly quoted definition of health is from Susruta. This work is unique in that it discusses blood in terms of the fourth doshic principle. This work is the first to enumerate and discuss the pitta sub-doshas. With its emphasis on pitta, surgery, and blood.
>
> **Michael Dick, who sells ayurvedic training tapes**

people willing to pay for a complete day of healing at an ayurvedic spa, which includes a little bit of yoga; a tasty vegetarian lunch; and three treatments, a massage, a facial, svedhana (medicated oil and steam and sauna), an ubvartan body scrub, or a reflexology footbath, all for around $200. The truly advanced ayurvedic healer will hire the hands-on help for minimum wage, leaving him- or herself free to sit back in their office and study the Gitas at leisure.

ß: Darned close to 200, unless you really believe in it, in which case you're not reading this book.

Skills Required: Spa management, avec un soupçon de Buddhism.

Duties: The ability to instill balance in unbalanced individuals.

Famous Examples: Bodhisattva Nagarjuna, a Buddhist philosopher, healer, and researcher of metallic alchemical medicines, generally considered responsible for bringing the important Avatamsaka Sutra to Earth after a visit to the Dragon Realm. Also Patch Adams, inspirational Western physician and subject of treacle-sweet movie starring Robin Williams.

How to Get It: The National Ayurvedic Medical Association suggests 500 hours of training. Master ayurvedic healers move upward into the field of herbalism, and the American Herbalists Guild suggests more than 1,600 hours for professional membership. Mail order degrees for the status of clinical ayurvedic therapist cost about $1,250.

The Upside: Not much competition since nobody knows what it is.

The Downside: Lots of sitting around involved, due to the focus on meditation. Too much discussion of sutras can become tedious.

The Dark Side: Extremely difficult to deal with people who believe they just returned from the Dragon Realm.

Where You Go from Here: Esalen, for a rest.

8

Backup Dancer

Dance behind people's behinds, provide controlled substances, marry pop tarts

$$: Depends on the divorce settlement and the quality of the prenup.

ß: 116.

Skills Required: Nice butt; look skanky for the tabloids, achieve good facial stubble; party on!

Duties: Order room service with aplomb; refrain from trashing hotel rooms until well after marriage; perform when required.

> As I mentioned before, I am now going to be expressing my personal life through art. This series will show us falling in love and all the adventures that went on overseas during the European leg of my Onyx Hotel tour. It's going to be an exciting ride. Kevin feels this project will speak for itself. Simply put, he says, "It is a documentation of love."
>
> **Britney Spears, on the now-defunct UPN series**

Famous Example: Kevin Federline defines the outer limits of this bullshit job. Aside from his reaching the post of stud and prince consort to Britney Spears, the nation's No. 1 pop tart of our day, Federline has a number of other achievements to his name. He is perhaps best known for being the seventeenth-billed dancer in what is, in some circles, considered the worst movie ever made, *You Got Served* (2004), starring, among others, J-Boog and Lil' Fizz. His greatest professional triumph to date took place after his nuptials, when he and Brit coproduced the UPN series *Britney & Kevin: Chaotic,* which repackaged their home videos for public scrutiny.

How to Get It: The basics are out by one online expert: "You have to take some dancing lessons with a profassional," he says, proving that spelling is not a requirement.

The Upside: Proximity to many talented people, one of whom may encounter you in an overheated condition and make a decision she will later regret and you will not.

The Downside: Having your Ferrari towed away by your pissed-off ex-wife.

The Dark Side: Looking at sleeping pop tart without makeup first thing in the morning.

Where You Go from Here: Restaurant greeter, Taco Bell.

9

Barista

Prepare doses for crazed acolytes of the bean

> A morning without coffee is like sleep.
>
> **Author unknown**

$$: Pretty lousy, starts at $7.75 per hour. Baristas make less by the hour than the kids who construct Double-Doubles at the In-N-Out—which are absolutely superb, by the way—who start at more than ten bucks an hour!

ß: 52. Sometimes you have to work too hard.

Skills Required: Nice smile. Ability to operate machinery, including cash register, possibly bake or microwave small, inedible but healthy pastry, without hurting oneself.

Duties: Grind beans, load filters, steam milk, dispense medication to addicts.

Famous Example: The team at Peet's Coffee in downtown Mill Valley, California. Hi, guys!

How to Get It: Fill out an application. Arrive sober.

The Upside: Beautiful, rich, sensuous coffee; coffee in beans in juicy, wildly odiferous blends; coffee roasting, dripping; hot milk frothing; and other human beings reaching out to you for the very thing that you can give them, plus free lattes for all your friends.

> Coffee leads men to trifle away their time, scald their chops, and spend their money, all for a little, base, thick, nasty, bitter, stinking, nauseous puddle water.
>
> **The Women's Petition Against Coffee, 1674**

The Downside: Deal with agitated, needy customers on the verge of a jag half the time.

The Dark Side: Poverty.

Where You Go from Here: Hand out medication in a mental institution.

10

Being a Brand

Become the personal embodiment of a product or service

$$: Untold millions.

ß: 45–101.

Skills Required: Must have achieved certain totemic status prior to assumption of brand identity.

> My first job came when I was four years old, and I sold painted rocks from my wagon.
>
> **Kathy Ireland**

Duties: Go dream up new ways to sell your name and image; wear large sunglasses, even at night.

Famous Examples: The original genius in this area was Walt Disney, who had the foresight and egomania to name every iteration of his vision for himself. More recently, Kathy Ireland, Martha Stewart, Jaclyn Smith, Mary-Kate and Ashley Olsen, each of whom appears on products in supermarkets that have nothing to do with what made them famous.

Also helps to be a doctor, as proven by Dr. Seuss, Dr. Scholl, Dr. Denton, Dr. J, Doc Marten, and Papa "Baby Doc" Duvalier.

How to Get It: Nobody has done more with what God gave her than swimsuit model Kathy Ireland.

She started out modeling for *Modern Bride* for $300 per day. Then she upgraded to cover girl for the legendary *Sports Illustrated* swimsuit issue. By 1993, she was marketing a line of "high-quality" socks under her name. Today, she has mutated into a "lifestyle designer" and motivational speaker, with a full line of objects—from candles to carpets, to home office products—that, when purchased, confer on their recipient the totality of the Kathy Ireland zeitgeist.

The Upside: See your name on people's butts as they walk down the street.

The Downside: Tacky people like your stuff.

The Dark Side: The horror of outliving one's brand.

Where You Go from Here: Kuala Lumpur, to oversee your sweatshops.

11

Being Donald Trump

Arguably the No. 1 bullshit artist on the planet

> One day of me is enough.
>
> **Donald Trump**

$$: No one really knows.

ß: 200 (the maximum allowable number).

Skills Required: Swaggering, primping, overstating; helps to have short, intense attention span and OCD-related issues like fear of handshaking.

Duties: Break a lot of wind, try to copyright the phrase, "You're fired," marry beauties from former Iron Curtain countries, sue people who write the truth about you.

Famous Example: Donald Trump.

How to Get It: Purport to be doing great no matter how things are actually going; borrow money when you need to.

The Upside: Your name is imprinted on everything you eat, live in, travel in, do your business in.

> If bullshit was music, that fellow would be a brass band.
>
> **Paddy Crosbie**

The Downside: Idiots make fun of your beautiful orange hair.

The Dark Side: Must refer to everybody as "Baby."

Where You Go from Here: The Bosley Institute.

12

Best-selling Author

Crank it out

> Writer's block is simply a failure of ego.
>
> **Norman Mailer**

$$: $500,000 and up, depending on royalties.

ß: 67–190, depending on how much of your books you actually write.

Skills Required: Attend celebratory cocktail parties without falling over; read drafts of your upcoming books when they force you to.

Duties: Cash checks.

Famous Example: James Patterson, some of whose recent books sport a second author in teeny-weeny type. Not that there's anything wrong with that.

How to Get It: It's important for every reader to recognize that bullshit jobs don't just up and fall into your lap from the start of your career as a working person. It is often necessary to work for years and years to reach the pinnacle of bullshit status, with its attendant easy lifestyle and ego-gratifying levels of fame and/or notoriety.

> It's not enough to succeed. Others must fail.
>
> **Gore Vidal**

This is nowhere more true than in the realm of best-selling authors, many of whom wrote good books for years before plunging into the pool of best-selling bullshit.

The Upside: Knowledge that one's name will live as long as there are airport bookstores.

The Downside: Mandatory rehab after you are arrested on the lawn of your Hamptons home dancing with a raw turkey.

The Dark Side: You can't start or finish anything without somebody else's "help."

Where You Go from Here: The Miami Book Fair.

13

Blogger

Download contents of your mind, even when there aren't any

> The trouble with the Internet is that it's replacing masturbation as a leisure activity.
>
> **Patrick Murray**

$$: Relatively small, but prospects for high-paying bullshit job in the future are virtually assured.

ß: 92. Sometimes you piss off the wrong people.

Skills Required: Ability to upload thoughts, vapors, resentments, insights, lack of insights, rumors, stuff you've heard, stuff you haven't heard, truth, lies, fiction, semifact, appropriated wisdom, logrolling, political and sociological venom, self-promotion, and other cultural effluvia on a blank screen day in and day out; must possess the impression that one's quotidian brain activity is of interest to others. Helps to be funny but when that is impossible, being hateful often suffices.

Duties: Write all day. Write all night. Doo-dah.

Famous Examples: Wonkette. All the blogs owned by Murdochian online minimogul Nick Denton—Defamer in LA, Gawker in New York—tend to be the crème de la crème of the genre, with vast knowledge of who is attractive and vulnerable to abuse. Others, like Matt Drudge and Jim Romenesko, are not bloggers per se but packagers of other people's digital farts and, at times, actual journalism.

How to Get It: Set up a Web log by establishing a site. That is your blank slate. Don't leave it blank for long. Start writing, and by writing, I mean filling up the screen with words. Try to do this all the time. Let no notion or twinge go unexplored. After a while, your natural human tendency to be appropriate or kind or thoughtful or to edit yourself in any way will decay, falling away from you like a dead husk. This is good. When it's gone altogether, you'll find your output will be staggering. It's not that hard to write when the activity itself is the only job requirement.

The Upside: This is one of the bullshit jobs you can do immediately, with no training and no prior experience. You can also become very famous, since the established media, increasingly devoid of excitement and ideas of its own, has taken to siphoning off daily blogging activity as a much better and more interesting alternative to actual news.

The Downside: You need a full, daily dose of imagination, guile, bile, and people pouring nonsense into your head that you can repeat.

The Dark Side: Your skin glows an ethereal white, your eyes become rheumy and bloodshot. Hair erupts in horrendous places. You don't care. You are now nothing but a conduit through which pass all the rare gases of the universe. You are, in short, a blog.

Where You Go from Here: McSweeney's.

14

Book Editor

Take breakfast meeting with writers, assign ideas generated by others, hound writers for manuscripts, have lunch, hound writers for manuscripts, have drinks and dinner. Repeat as necessary.

$$: $16,000–$450,000, depending. The lower you are paid, the less bullshit your job is; conversely, the more you make, the more access you have to the highest, rocket-grade bullshit imaginable.

> No passion in the world is equal to the passion to alter someone else's draft.
>
> **H. G. Wells**

ß: 15–104. What a range! Entry-level editors must rewrite and proofread manuscripts (like one this instance for), and field angry phone calls from authors and agents so that their bosses can talk to other people with bullshit jobs (see Best-selling Author).

Skills Required: There are still some book editors around who actually mark up manuscripts, but the truly successful ones wouldn't risk inkstains on their Armani cuffs. The great ones operate in pure ideas and conjecture—like which to order for lunch at Michael's: the sweetbreads or the Cobb salad? Occasionally, they will weigh into the process by barking, "Where's my book!" The great book editor is at once a gifted salesperson, an arbiter of taste, a babysitter of lost souls, and a closet boulevardier. God bless them, both of them.

Duties: Ability to "read" a 300-page book before lunch, while answering e-mails on his BlackBerry.

Famous Example: Maxwell Perkins, a towering figure of the 1920s and '30s, whose aggressive yet thoughtful shaping of the great modern authors like F. Scott Fitzgerald and Thomas Wolfe, hewed solid monuments of literature out of flaccid, egotistical lumps of prose. The fact that Maxwell Perkins existed has made it possible for generations of book editors who came after him to feel good about their profession.

How to Get It: Take a job for no money upon graduating from an Ivy League school; live at your parents' house for three years until you make a living wage; then inherit a best-selling exercise book from an editor who's left for a better bullshit job.

The Upside: Meet Oprah.

The Downside: You are seated with James Frey and Nan Talese at the PEN dinner.

The Dark Side: Must eat at Elaine's.

Where You Go from Here: Elaine's.

15

Boulevardier

Frequent the most fashionable places, enjoy the company of fatuous people who are impressed with you and use your social cachet as their own, or vice versa

> I will not date a depressed woman. I want to have fun.
>
> **George Hamilton**

$$: None. Being a boulevardier is an ancillary bullshit occupation that must feed off a core job that produces income. The premier boulevardier of our time, George Hamilton, acts to support his tan and his bon vivant lifestyle; his activities as a boulevardier in turn enhance his chances to obtain appropriate roles satirizing himself.

ß: 158.

Skills Required: Charm, ability to sponge without shame.

Duties: Dress well, speak a few languages, bleach teeth, be able to hold an infinite amount of liquor (!), know how to dance like a white man, remain on excellent terms with ex-lovers and wives, look elegant, produce short bursts of scintillating conversation.

Famous Examples: In addition to George Hamilton? Jay McInerney (used to be a wunderkind), Henry Kissinger (used to be a war criminal), Tommy Lee (used to be sort-of interesting).

How to Get It: Must be good-looking and have achieved a certain level of celebrity already, but not enough to make people uncomfortable. Beyond that, all that's required is showing up, over and over again, and always looking like you're having fun.

The Upside: Barry Diller always says hello.

The Downside: Secret knowledge of one's own fatuosity.

The Dark Side: Skin cancer.

Where You Go from Here: I don't know. Where's the party?

16

Business Book Author

Make poor slobs feel more in control

$$: Good to Great!

ß: Freakazoidinal.

Skills Required: Must be able to write very short chapters that prey on insecurities of working people.

Duties: Write book. Watch money roll in.

Famous Example: Spencer Johnson, whose book *Who Moved My Cheese?* stands as a testament to all that this book is trying to achieve. It is the story of a tiny mouse who realizes that all his problems in life are created by his unwillingness to take personal responsibility for

Many years ago, Dr. Spencer Johnson was having a difficult time dealing with a major change in his life. He thought it wasn't fair, and he was confused and angry... So he made up the story of *Who Moved My Cheese?* to get him to laugh at himself, with his follies and fears, and to encourage him to change, move on and realize something better. He kept the story to himself and lived it until he found "New Cheese."

From the moving story of *Who Moved My Cheese?*

his cheese. Sounds dumb, huh? But when this object in your hands is steadying the leg of a chair somewhere, that stupid thing will still be flying off the shelves.

How to Get It: Whether your book is designed to make the reader feel just a little smarter than he did before he read it, or to instruct him in some wise, essential points that anyone with common sense would know, you'll need to write very, very simply and in such a way that people who have no desire to read your book will talk about it. Also—must have a good title, like this book.

The Upside: Make huge bucks giving the same speech for thirty years.

The Downside: You have fraudulently purported to be able to help people manage that which is unmanageable. Shame on you!

The Dark Side: Macadamia nuts in your Ritz-Carlton minibar can't be expensed.

Where You Go from Here: *Charlie Rose.*

17

Cable News Demagogue

Deliver highly opinionated news and views to people who don't want to hear anything that disagrees with them

$$: $20 million per year.

ß: Incalculable, due to size of income and intensity of bullshit.

Skills Required: Talk talk talk. Be irate. Attack anybody who disagrees with you. Call them traitors. Know the difference between a falafel and a loofah.

Duties: Blow up a big fat balloon every day.

Famous Example: Bill O'Reilly.

> So anyway, I'd be rubbing your big boobs and getting your nipples really hard, kinda kissing your neck from behind . . . and then I would take the other hand with the falafel thing and I'd just put it on your pussy but then you'd have to do it really light, just kind of a tease business.
>
> **From the sexual harassment lawsuit filed against Bill O'Reilly by Andrea MacKris, a former producer of his show**

How to Get It: "If you are honest, work hard, and try to help others when you can, then good things will happen to you. Life is full of little surprises." In this statement, as in so many others, Bill O'Reilly shows others that when it comes to the fine art of bullshitting, he is without peer. Let's look at his inspirational story.

> And guys, if you exploit a girl, it will come back to you. That's called "karma."
>
> Bill O'Reilly, *The O'Reilly Factor for Kids,* 2004

O'Reilly started at a small TV station in Scranton, Pennsylvania, for $150 a week, and augmented his income writing promotional spin and interstitial dialogue for *Uncle Ted's Monster Fest,* the station's Saturday late-night horror movie. At the same time, he was sending his quirky news pods to ABC News in New York, which was impressed and aired some of them. From there he went to Dallas, then Denver, where he won an Emmy covering a skyjacking, and then to the New York local CBS affiliate, where he won another Emmy for investigative reporting. From there, he ascended to the position of anchor at the CBS and ABC affiliates in Boston and a whole bunch of other big accomplishments before joining Fox in 1996, including receiving an MA in public policy from that great spin factory, Harvard's Kennedy School of Government.

In 1996, he asserted his right to turn his chosen profession into a bullshit job, and it is, in fact, through that very transformation that the society in which we live and work has awarded him the highest levels of success and remuneration.

> Patriotism is the last refuge of the scoundrel.
>
> **Samuel Johnson, 1775**

The heart of O'Reilly's bullshit is in his mastery of the fact that there is tremendous power in asserting what is obviously false as true. Thus O'Reilly's television program, *all* spin, is known as the "No Spin Zone." Brutal, mean, and impressively full of it, he is a tower of bullshit achievement. Next to him, lightweights like Geraldo and Sean Hannity look like Ben Franklin.

The Upside: Pleasure of vanquishing the small and weak.

The Downside: Must occasionally listen to other people talk.

The Dark Side: Develop tendency to spew insane nonsense when exercised, like "If Al Qaeda comes in here and blows you up, we're not going to do anything about it. We're going to say, look, every other place in America is off-limits to you, except San Francisco."

Where You Go from Here: Explode in a conflagration of boiling fat.

18

Celebrity Stylist/ Aesthetic Consultant

Create a look for people who want to be looked at

> He completely gets my body.
>
> **Kristin Chenoweth on LA designer Kevan Hall**

$$: Good bucks with no security whatsoever. If you lose your mojo, you might as well go back to Boise.

ß: 85–108; it's all about whose bullshit prevails, particularly if you're dressing Kathy Griffin.

Skills Required: Overpowering personality capable of forcing insecure people to adopt your vision of themselves. Must be thin and absolutely fabulous by the standard set five minutes ago. Ultimate goal is to enable clients to look completely individual and, at the same time, totally predictable.

Duties: Attend catwalk shows, red carpets, openings, closings, photo shoots; carry Crest Whitestrips for dental whiteness emergencies; appear on E! Channel with at least one of the surgically reconstructed Rivers.

> Every time I see a photo of myself from the past month, I think, "What was I thinking?"
>
> **Chloë Sevigny**

Famous Examples: Rachel Zoe (Rosenzweig), who makes up to $6,000 per day dressing, among others, Lindsay Lohan, Nicole Richie, and Jessica Simpson; Phillip Bloch, who does John Travolta, Salma Hayek, and Jada Pinkett Smith; and of course John Derek, who, with his wife Bo, took the field to the highest level since Pygmalion kissed Galatea.

How to Get It: Simply fall into the position from a world that naturally breeds fashion ideas, like hip-hop or prison.

The Upside: Everybody wants to be your baby.

The Downside: When your client makes the Worst Dressed List.

The Dark Side: You wake up one morning and look like Bruce Vilanch.

Where You Go from Here: Kmart, for all the marbles.

19

Celebutante

Be fabulous and scandalous and famous and hot!

$$: Millions for endorsements and everything is on the house! That's hot.

ß: 103 degrees. That's hot.

> Times are bad. Children no longer listen to their parents, and everyone is writing a book.
>
> **Cicero, Circa 66 B.C.**

Skills Required: Look good; don't give a shit; willingness to change color of hair and eyes daily.

Duties: Be slim, don't lose cellular Sidekick, carry small dog, do stuff in bathroom stalls.

Famous Examples: Paris Hilton, and then everyone else. Genius comes in all shapes and forms, and hers is something special.

How to Get It: Go anywhere, do anything, never let anybody harsh your glow. Be hot.

> Cockroaches and socialites are the only things that can stay up all night and eat anything.
>
> **Herb Caen**

The Upside: The cover of *Vanity Fair!*

The Downside: Daily bikini waxing, in case paparazzi catch you without underwear. Come to think of it, you never wear underwear!

The Dark Side: Sleazy sex partner captures you on videotape and sells your stoned, dazed, humping, raccoon-eyed act all over the world. No, wait a minute! That's the upside!

Where You Go from Here: Carl's Jr., for breakfast.

20

Certified Massage Therapist

Rub other people the right way

$$: $70–$100 an hour, as long as you don't end up on your back; then it's more.

ß: 25–56. It's a lot of work, and you have to put up with a lot of bullshit.

Skills Required: Strong, smooth hands; no hangnails; good breath.

> I'm sure that your intentions are good, but I'm not comfortable with that. So please take your hands off me.
>
> **Anonymous masseuse, Marin County, CA, where, according to one poll, one in five supermarket shoppers is a certified massage therapist**

Duties: Increase relaxation and blood flow in others, but only in appropriate body parts.

Famous Example: Phoebe from *Friends.*

How to Get It: Get certified, which often takes between 135 and 1,000 hours. After certification, advanced bullshit artists may extend the job into reiki, energy work, polarity, crystal massage, and other wanky stuff that hauls in the gullible and jacks up the price.

The Upside: A terrific icebreaker when you meet people at a party.

The Downside: You have to put up with clients saying things like, "Yes! Yes! Deeper! Deeper! More! More!" Plus, everybody always wants free massages.

The Dark Side: Depending on your appearance, you have to tell between 5 percent and 20 percent of your clients that you're not interested in providing them with "lymphatic drainage."

Where You Go from Here: Professional dog walker.

21

Chairman

Visionary, autocrat, delegator

> I am not a paranoid deranged millionaire, goddammit. I'm a billionaire.
>
> **Howard Hughes**

$$: You're beyond the point where you need money. Money is for people who move through space in a world not of their making. That's not you.

ß: It really depends on how you're feeling. Every once in a while, you must deliver something not bullshit based, and that makes up for all the bullshit you've heaped on the planet at all other times. But not too often, OK?

Skills Required: Make pronouncements; hear without listening; have vision when required.

Duties: Preside over meetings at which your mere presence guarantees that nothing of substance is discussed.

Famous Examples: Augustus Caesar. Mao Tse-tung. Howard Hughes. Frank Sinatra.

> They are able because they think they are able.
>
> **Virgil**

How to Get It: You have always been a different kind of duck. Led when others had no idea what to do. You were at once the most necessary and most obnoxious person in any group. Actually, you never were of the group, even when you were surrounded by it. Every chance you had to advance, whether by peaceful means or by the annihilation of your enemy, you seized it. You have always, in a sense, been the chairman, even before you got the title. Now that you are functionally insane, any self-doubts you used to have are completely evaporated and you are free! Free! Hahahaha!!!

The Upside: Your feet do not touch the floor when you walk. This saves money on shoes.

The Downside: The voices in your head won't let you sleep at night.

The Dark Side: Everything is crawling with germs, and nobody knows how to clean your bottom without leaving it all red and chafed.

Where You Go from Here: Cryogenic Freezing.

22

Cheese Artisan

Sculpt milk products for upscale restaurants and pretentious markets

> Poets have been mysteriously silent on the subject of cheese.
>
> **G. K. Chesterton**

$$: Virtually unlimited for those who craft museum-quality work.

ß: 73.8, since the number is reduced when people actually eat what you make, rendering it useful.

Skills Required: Must be able to make simple cheese worthy of critical attention.

Duties: Making cheese and cheese products is only the beginning. From there, the artisanal cheese professional moves into the area where the *fromage* is honed, sculpted, packaged, and presented in a manner that makes all other cheese look like Velveeta.

Famous Example: Sid Cook, from the fourth generation of cheese artisans who operate the Carr Valley Cheese

Company's factory, located on County Truck Highway G in La Valle, Wisconsin. Sid got his cheese-making license at age sixteen, an age when most people don't even know that a license is required to make cheese.

> Blessed are the cheese makers.
>
> **Monty Python**

How to Get It: This is a field in which naïfs and talented amateurs can rise to the top, especially those who work in Edam, Gruyère, dill-infused Havarti, or other alternative media.

The Upside: The knowledge that people really love what you do, especially with crackers.

The Downside: Critics don't take you seriously just because you work in cheese.

The Dark Side: Mold!

Where You Go from Here: Smoked meat artisan.

23

Closet Organizer

Organize closets for people who can't organize their own closets

> One of the first tips I give clients is to use the same hanger for all your clothes—this allows you to see everything clearly and focus solely on the clothes.
>
> **Melanie Charlton, closet organizer**

$$: Middling, unless the closet belongs to some crazy rich person, and who else would hire a closet organizer?

ß: 99.

Skills Required: Some color coordination, decent feel for spatial relations, good technique with hangers.

Duties: Soothe nutty, confused person. Gain her trust, or his trust if you're dealing with a male homosexual. Move into closet, winnowing out ugly stuff, thinning out the underbrush. Mandate decent hangers, solid shoe storage solution, proper use of overhead areas. Take your time. This isn't meant to look easy. When you're finished with the main closet opportunities, discuss such important line extensions as mudrooms, garages, and basements. Be creative. You are there to tend to a troubled soul in need of arrangement.

Famous Example: Who cares?

How to Get It: Start with friends, the way Tupperware or encyclopedia salespeople do. Then move outward in concentric circles to ensnare all the loopy, unwound souls you can find.

The Upside: Unparalleled opportunity for those with an unhealthy interest in footwear.

The Downside: Hard to explain what you do to serious people, and therefore you may not find yourself around many.

The Dark Side: Obsessive-compulsive disorder acquired over time degenerates into horrible need to keep everything on matching hangers, followed shortly by madness and death.

Where You Go from Here: Stager, another bullshit job, where people set up an apartment that's for sale to look more attractive than it actually is.

24

Cold Caller

Honk on the phone all day, trying to sell people things they don't need

$$: Piddling. But oh, the freedom from thought! The lack of expectations! If hope, as the Zen masters say, is suffering, this is a job without any of either.

ẞ: 75.

Skills Required: Strong index finger; tolerance for being sworn at and hung up on.

> Good morning. This is ________________ from Career Blazers. I'd like to ask you a question. (Pause.) Do you have any temporary needs today?
>
> **Script of pitch selling temps to businesses who didn't need them, circa 1980**

Duties: Call people. Repeat scripted pitch. Call people. Repeat scripted pitch. Go home. Shoot self (optional).

Famous Example: Me.

How to Get It: Answer a want ad. Or just walk in.

In the latter part of the twentieth century, I took a break from my successful career as an actor and strolled into the offices of Career Blazers, a firm that blazed careers for unemployed people who were willing to do anything at that point to make a buck. They took me into a back room where eight human beings of various shapes and sizes were pounding on the phone, selling the company's temps. They gave me a script, a desk, and a pitch. The customary answer to "Do you have any temporary needs today?" was "No! But I've got some permanent ones you could probably help me with!" followed by hilarious laughter and a click. I made $87.50 a week, plus commissions, of which there were exactly none. The office manager was a guy who sat in a tiny outer office, staring into space and drinking coffee. He would be sitting there still if we all had not been fired en masse about three months into my term of employment, for the simple reason that together we had produced no revenue.

The Upside: You don't have to dress up for work (or dress at all, for that matter, if you work from home); random phone sex with low-level HR operatives.

The Downside: People really hate you.

The Dark Side: You stink.

Where You Go from Here: You become a person who has to talk to cold callers when they interrupt your dinner because you've been there and know what it's like to be treated rudely.

25

Computer Game Tester

Frag zombies

$$: $40,000 per year, tons of free software, and state-of-the-art gear.

> A good tester is like a bulldog . . . tenaciously digging his teeth into a bug and not letting go until he figures it out.
>
> **Tom Sloper, Sloperama Productions**

ß: 44. Surprisingly low, I know, but keep in mind that you have to keep some records of the games you are playing for defects, possible improvements, monsters that walk through virtual walls when they shouldn't, imps that refuse to die no matter how many times you shoot them with the plasma gun.

Skills Required: Great hand-eye coordination and a willingness to sit in front of a computer screen for twenty-four hours a day without turning into a blob, or at least not minding it when you do.

Duties: Play games, report quirks and bugs, smoke weed.

Famous Examples: Back in the old days, before gaming got corporatized, there were madmen who programmed their own games, tested them, put them up as shareware, and made history. For me the greatest will always be John Romero, whose id Software was the author of the great first-person shooter games of the 1990s—Wolfenstein 3D and Doom. Thanks, John, for all those wasted hours.

How to Get It: Never listen to anybody who tells you that you're losing your eyesight and turning your brain into cream cheese. Listen to them, and you could end up with another bullshit job that's a lot harder to do and at the bottom of the heap in terms of fun (see Lawyer).

The Upside: Naked chicks bursting out of their tiny tees!

The Downside: Zits.

The Dark Side: You sink into the universe created in a new massive multiplayer online role-playing game and never come out.

Where You Go from Here: The planet Vrod III, where mutant zogs are attacking the starbase and a BFG is called for.

26

Construction Site Flag Waver

Stand in street and cause confusion

> If you want a place in the sun, you've got to put up with a few blisters.
>
> **Abigail Van Buren**

$$: Minimum wage for municipal construction crew, which turns out to be more than many employees make at corporate jobs.

ß: 90. Sometimes it's too cold or too hot out.

Skills Required: Strong upper torso for heavy traffic periods; must look good in orange and stripes and be able to remain on feet for long periods of time without passing out.

Duties: Stand at "active" road construction zones and wave traffic away from the guys who are chatting, having coffee and a smoke before they go back to chatting, smoking, and having coffee.

Famous Examples: Ed. Also Bob.

How to Get It: It helps to know a guy who knows a guy. After that, you're in. You will never stop "working." I personally have seen flag-waving and chin-wagging road construction sites in New York, Chicago, St. Louis, San Francisco, and Los Angeles for twenty and thirty years with no indication of what the hell they're doing. And still the flags are waved by the guy who, I believe, volunteered for that duty solely out of the desire to have some fun driving motorists crazy. This is, in short, bullshit at its most aggressive and, for those with the proper frame of mind, satisfying.

The Upside: Wave drivers on cell phones into a ditch.

The Downside: You're the only one working at the site. That's really not fair.

The Dark Side: Lots of exhaust in your face.

Where You Go from Here: NFL ref.

27

Consultant

Have gun, will travel

$$: Entry level grunts may begin in the high five and low six figures. If you're a graduate of one of the huge consultant factories that leach humanity out of students and turn them into guns for hire—Wharton, and to a lesser extent, the somewhat squishier Stanford School of Business—you could be making an executive's salary almost immediately.

> His peculiarities caused him to be invited to every house; all wished to see him, and those who had been accustomed to violent excitement, and now felt the weight of ennui, were pleased at having something in their presence capable of engaging their attention.
>
> ***The Vampyre*, John Polidori**

ß: 50–150.

Skills Required: Must be a champ at managing up. I was at a meeting with a bloated toad of a consultant a decade or so ago. Complete troll. Knew nothing. Didn't wear socks with his Weejuns. Nautical brass buttons on his blazer. We sat down, the president of my division and I, we who were being acquired, and spent about ten minutes running him through the realities of the business, its pitfalls, its various constituencies. He nodded judiciously, picked lightly at some scabrous tissue at the edge of his earlobe, and said, "Who is responsible for paying my bill?" Then he made a quick phone call, and we were instantly joined by one of those android junior nerdlinger types who seem pressed out of foam board. At that time in history, it was permissible for younger consultants to have a tiny soul patch below their lower lip, so he had one. "I want Mike to be fully briefed as well," said the sockless boss dude. From that time forth, we dealt with Mike. The big gasbag worked directly with the chairman, because he was the one who cut the checks.

Duties: Chopper in. Get your orders. Receive validation from senior officer, one that allows you to push staff people around a little bit. Schedule meetings in which people are forced to talk about things they probably would rather not. "Capture" the "findings" in big pieces of paper you post on the walls during the meeting. "Drill deep" into "process" with employees. Identify "challenges and opportunities" and "reach for new solutions." Go off. Have several glasses of malbec. Write "findings," telling your client a mixture of the things he needs to hear, the things he wants to hear, and the stuff you tell everybody. Go home. Feel good, having left the problems you solved and the problems you created behind you.

Famous Example: Gershon Kekst, the elderly, avuncular Yoda who runs his own communications and crisis management agency. Big companies who have a problem call Kekst, get Kekst, have a meeting with Kekst at which he is warm, wise, and wonderful. Everybody feels much better. The problem doesn't go away, really, but management can say they are working with Kekst. By the way, unless something is very wrong indeed, that is probably the last time anybody concerned sees Kekst, except for the Kekst family, possibly.

How to Get It: I hate to tell you this, but the best route to consultancy is business school. The good news is that, unlike medical or law school, this involves a level of bullshit that any reader of this volume will find easily achievable.

The Upside: It's a pretty easy job, with great travel benefits, nice hotels, drinks on the companies you are soaking.

The Downside: Your kids can never explain what you do to their friends.

The Dark Side: You are a ninja, a samurai, a lone traveler on the road to nowhere. It's a very opulent nowhere if you're good at it. But somewhere in your heart, you want to come in from the cold.

Where You Go from Here: Seat 3H in first class. Get to the Glenlivet fast because it goes quick.

28

Contractor

Manage subcontractors, leave when job is 75 percent done

> It's good to be the king.
>
> **Mel Brooks**

$$: Whoa, Nellie. If you take on and incompletely serve a full complement of clients, you can really clean up.

ß: 37. All the bullshit here is in the endgame, compared to other jobs that are shot through and through with it from beginning to end (see Economist).

Skills Required: You have to be able to walk around with your hands on your hips in an evaluating fashion and give an estimate in such a way that when you blow by it later by, say, 75 percent, nobody is really very mad at you. Believe me, that kind of bullshitting is hard to learn and even harder to carry off without being assaulted.

The true job of a contractor is to manage a large team of illegal immigrant workers and craftsmen, getting them to work quickly and well up to the point where the job is almost complete. By then, you should have accomplished one of the key skills of any bullshit professional in this regard—getting paid.

Duties: Now is when the true job of the contractor kicks in—putting off the least profitable and most aggravating part of any job: finishing it. For here is where the average customer is a total pain, demanding niceties, like molding where you said it was going to be, or touch-ups to the paint job you ruined when you moved in the stove, and a host of other time-consuming activities that make you far less in profit than the first 80 percent of the job has done. You've got to do the absolute minimum, stalling and stalling until the poor client gives up and does whatever you want just to end the pain of associating with you. In this way, your work is not unlike that of the successful divorce attorney.

Famous Example: Vince Mancuso, who did my house in the 1990s. Most of what he did was great, and what he didn't finish doesn't matter anyhow. He only exceeded his estimate by 20 percent, so that wasn't so bad. The day we didn't have to deal with him anymore was one of the greatest days of liberation since the Allies marched into Paris in 1945, which I was too young to see. Important note: His name was not really Vince Mancuso or anything like it. I don't want any contractors of that name coming to my house and shooting me with a gun like the one the real

Vince Mancuso (which is not his name) kept in his glove compartment.

How to Get It: This in its essence is a management job. The successful contractor doesn't do work, per se, not after a while. He hires people who know how to do it and then keeps an eye on the pace of things and the costs associated, scares up new business, takes home most of the gravy. He's the boss. Nothing better than that.

The Upside: Bag the occasional wife.

The Downside: If you aggravate enough people, you have to go back to being a subcontractor, and there's nothing bullshit about that.

The Dark Side: A few years ago I was driving up my street, and about two blocks away I passed by a house that was burning down. The family that had bought it had hired a contractor to gut it, put in a new roof, fix it up, and give it to them on time. A week before they were to move in, the place was far from being in any liveable condition, so the subcontractors were working around the clock, including the guy who was supposed to do electrical, who it turned out later wasn't really licensed. So on the Friday before the Monday the family was supposed to take possession, the crew decided to knock off early, their boss being decamped from the scene. The electrical guy left something running, and a spark set the new roof on fire because it was being coated with something flammable, due to the fact that time was short and everything had to be done at once. And the roof caught and made a merry blaze, and when it was all over the only thing left standing was the Port-A-Potty.

Where You Go from Here: Project manager, Kennedy Airport reconstruction project.

29

Corporate Yes-Man

Help senior management feel good about itself

> I don't want any yes-men around me. I want everyone to tell me the truth—even if it costs him his job.
>
> **Sam Goldwyn**

$$: $27,500–$1.5 million and up.

ß: 60.

Skills Required: Much more difficult than it appears to be. A true yes-man must listen carefully to the thoughts and opinions of his or her bosses and triangulate which opinions are important enough to be agreed with. Indiscriminate yessing engenders disrespect and mistrust, just as maladroit sucking up can ruin the credibility of a perfectly good middle manager and make subsequent brownnosing and tuft hunting ineffective. Faux agreement is a highly orchestrated and subtle form of bullshit, and should not be handled by the inexperienced, shallow, or dense.

Duties: Telling nabobs of one size or another what they want to hear without having them come to the conclusion that you are a despicable, untrustworthy, worthless moron whose opinions have no validity whatsoever. To use agreement as a strategic tool that helps your superior feel good about doing the right things, and to achieve your own personal goals by doing so.

> The basis of optimism is sheer terror.
>
> **Oscar Wilde**

Famous Examples: H. R. Haldeman, who worked for Richard Nixon and agreed with him all the way to impeachment; the guys who worked for Howard Hughes, who yessed him to the point where they are said to have decided, as a group, to put him out of his misery with a lethal injection; Harriet Miers, who never heard an opinion from George W. Bush that she didn't find absolutely brilliant.

How to Get It: Deploy a protostrategy of yessing at the job interview. Quiz your potential employer about a number of key issues, and at critical points initiate the first phase of any yesmanship—nodding. After nodding come small exclamations of accord, after which, if they are accepted with even moderate pleasure, more substantial statements of support. If you are hired after this, you know that you have a senior manager who is susceptible to judicious agreement. After that, less is more. It is unwise to disagree too often or too strenuously, but an occasional demurral is permissible, as is a strong, vocal voicing of opinions on issues the boss has yet to claim or opine about. This is wide latitude indeed in many cases, and one that is rarely explored by craven yes-men who give the entire bullshit approach a bad name.

The Upside: Effective yessing gives you the right to speak your mind when you have one.

The Downside: You must occasionally lose at golf to men who play worse than you do.

The Dark Side: Utter public humiliation. At a staff meeting a long time ago, the then-president of the company was seated next to our then-chairman, Dan, a scary guy who didn't like to be contradicted. The problem was, Dan didn't always share his opinion on things before requisitioning yours, and if you came up with the wrong one, his pupils got very tiny and the rest of his iris spread out to occupy his entire eyeball. It was not a pretty sight. So anyhow, the president, we'll call him Bill, was sitting there minding his own business, and Dan turns to him and says, "About that Baltimore thing, Bill, what do you think about it?" And Bill sits there like a total dummy, and then he says, "I think whatever you think, Dan." And the whole table, after a beat, cracks up. Ooh. You don't want that to happen.

Where You Go from Here: FEMA.

30

Critic

Suck thumb for big bucks

$$: Not very much. This relative poverty, compared to many of the authors, filmmakers, and other artists whose work they pass judgment on, sometimes makes them harsh, bitter, vindictive, petty, vicious, unpleasant, and unattractive. Did I mention hateful?

> Critics are like eunuchs in a harem; they know how it's done, they've seen it done every day, but they're unable to do it themselves.
>
> **Brendan Behan**

ß: 25–175.

Skills Required: Must be able to toss those pucks around at any length.

Duties: Project your own tastes, notions, and hopes for our larger civilization onto some creative person who is attempting to make a buck.

Famous Examples: Edmund Wilson, a tremendous writer and artist in his own right, whose voluminous journals and works of criticism have outlived much of the musty stuff he was assigned to write about. Frank Rich of *The New York Times,* whose blatant, fawning Anglophilia virtually destroyed American playwriting in the 1980s.

> The only reviewer who ever made an impression on me was Skabichevsky, who prophesied that I would die in the bottom of a ditch.
>
> **Anton Chekhov**

How to Get It: The thing is, if you were going to be a bullshit critic, you would pretty much know it already. You would have begun fomenting nasty, pointed diatribes in your student newspaper a long time ago. You would be comfortable telling people what you thought of movies you haven't even seen yet.

The Upside: People fear and spit shine you all the time, even though for the most part it will do them no good.

The Downside: All your friends are critics.

The Dark Side: A while ago, my friend Stanley ran into the guy who killed his book in *The New York Times.* He punched him in the nose.

Where You Go from Here: Wherever it is, you're not completely happy with it.

31

Crumber

Remove detritus from dining tables in restaurants

> Life is what you do while you're out making other plans.
>
> **John Lennon**

$$: $5.50 per hour, more if you get a piece of the tips.

ß: 100.

Skills Required: Must wield decrumbing implement.

Duties: Wait until exact right moment during the meal being enjoyed by others, swoop in, decrumb. Go back to corner and wait for next opportunity.

Famous Examples: To be found at the nearest little theater near you or at your local art gallery, lurking around outside with a portfolio in her hands, or shivering on a street corner waiting for a chance to get inside the studio and sing for somebody. The most famous, in my experience, is actress/model Gretchen Mol, who was checking coats at Michael's restaurant one day and on the cover of *Vanity Fair* the next.

How to Get It: Look around you. They're everywhere—people who must take crumby jobs while they are waiting for something else to come along to lift them up and out.

The Upside: Get to use cool tool and eat leftovers.

The Downside: Waste of life.

The Dark Side: Get to like crumbing, as opposed to auditioning.

Where You Go from Here: LA, if you know what's good for you.

32

Customer Service Representative, Canned Food Company

Take complaints, apologize when there are no maraschino cherries in the fruit cocktail, compensate with coupons

$$: About $20,000 a year, unless you are part-time.

ß: 48–123, since while the problems people present are generally bullshit, your solutions are not. How many beefs can be resolved with a couple of coupons for free cans of fruit salad? If the whole world could be healed that way, what a better place it would be!

> **Q:** There's a slug in my creamed corn.
>
> **A:** I'm sending you a coupon for six free cans.
>
> **Q:** Wow! Great, man! Thanks!
>
> **Actual conversation between complaining caller and customer affairs representative**

Skills Required: Must be good at dealing with angry people who require a real solution to a bullshit problem.

Duties: Receive multiple telephone calls and e-mails complaining about the product, ascertain solutions, and implement them so that the issues, and the people, go away. Look for better job.

Famous Example: My friend Ted, who did it for a while and then moved on to selling linoleum glue over the phone.

How to Get It: Like many who need a job but are not yet interested in a career, Ted parachuted into a whole bunch of wanky employment situations through a temp agency that sent him out to explore the great and disturbing unknown, which remains unknown, I believe, for a reason. This was just one of many opportunities he was given to do a bunch of bullshit for a little bit of money. Another time he went to a legal firm whose department wasn't expecting him, so he was given the job of pasting name tags on plastic binders. Another time, he chauffeured around a bunch of Asian businessmen who were mad that he didn't know how to fix them up with cocktail waitresses.

The Upside: Make your own hours. Always different. Seldom boring. Easy exit.

The Downside: Makes you never want to eat canned fruit again.

The Dark Side: Somebody finds a finger in their peaches.

Where You Go from Here: Back to school, for a career in market research.

33

Diet Doctor

Inspire fat people to buy books

> The biggest seller is cookbooks and the second is diet books—how not to eat what you've just learned how to cook.
>
> **Andy Rooney**

$$: On its lowest levels, which they call a nutritionist, it's still pretty good, well into the mid-$100,000 level, since very needy people with low self-esteem will flock to you and never leave. At the guru level (see Guru), the money is excellent, and if you have a successful book you are truly in fat city.

ß: 99.

Skills Required: Repackage old wisdom in designer jeans.

Duties: On a personal level, meet with fat people and listen to why their fatness is not related to what they eat, even though you both know otherwise. Discuss at length your own personal philosophy (note: get a personal philosophy). Brainwash client into accepting your philosophy. Counsel client during painful process of getting thin. Avoid hatred of client when all the weight is gained back. Refer client to surgeon you know for permanent results.

> I've decided that perhaps I'm bulimic and just keep forgetting to purge.
>
> **Paula Poundstone**

Famous Examples: Dr. Herman Tarnower, author of the Scarsdale Diet, which died when he did at the hands of his former lover, Jean Harris, the headmistress of a posh DC-area private academy. Dr. Atkins, whose low-carb diet really works until you go quietly insane and begin dreaming of toast.

How to Get It: The job you really want here is not diet doctor, of course, it's ghostwriter.

The Upside: Money. Sex. Power.

The Downside: Can never eat a Ring Ding without looking over your shoulder.

The Dark Side: Posthumous decline in your book sales, particularly if you die under fat circumstances.

Where You Go from Here: Cabo San Lucas.

34

Dolphin Trainer

Get aquatic mammals to smile for Kodak moments

$$: Decent.

ß: 65.

Skills Required: Must look good in wet suit.

Duties: Performs and oversees fish catching, netting, and removal of sea life from lagoons; trains staff for manatee rescue team; participates in animal necropsy.

Famous Example: Mitzi, who played the original Flipper in the 1960s television series. Wait a minute. That was the dolphin.

They call him Flipper,
Flipper, faster than lightning,
No-one you see, is
smarter than he,
And we know Flipper,
lives in a world full of wonder,
Flying there-under, under
the sea!

Theme song of original *Flipper* TV show, September 1964–April 1967

How to Get It: The applicant must be diver certified, physically fit and able to lift seventy-five pounds, work well with animals, repair gear, and have a clean driving record. The job itself isn't actually all that bullshitty. But the years of hanging around being a diver qualifies this one for the list.

The Upside: Play with Flipper or Mitzi or whomever.

The Downside: Necropsy. That can't be good.

The Dark Side: Must deal with Zipper, Flipper's legendary evil twin.

Where You Go from Here: See Aquarium Cleaner for the Rich.

35

Economist

Generate conflicting opinions

> I guess I should warn you, if I turn out to be particularly clear, you've probably misunderstood what I've said.
>
> **Alan Greenspan**

$$: Academics make professors' salaries, in the high five or low six figures. Those who work for Wall Street firms or other fiduciary institutions can make enough to force Eliot Spitzer to sit up and take notice.

ß: 128.

Skills Required: Write very poorly, or at least so obliquely that no matter what happens in reality, the theories and prognostications you offer can never be called wrong, exactly.

Duties: Teach. Study global trends. Think about the relationship between markets and monetary phenomena. Embrace and/or construct economic theories that fit with your political leanings. For instance, liberal economists tend to focus on aspects of the macrosystem that bolster a belief in working people and their rights in the face of the powers that run the means of production; conservative economists like free markets that allow rich people to get richer without worrying about the effect that may have on others.

Famous Examples: Paul Krugman of *The New York Times* because he's obviously very smart and open about his political stance on things, and uses economics quite brilliantly to bolster arguments that I agree with.

How to Get It: Really hard. Must go to college, then grad school, then get a PhD, which is a totally bullshit exercise except that you have to write a thesis. Only after all of that do you get to be a real economist. Then you have to find a place to be an economist in which they will pay you for it. As with being a film director, you can't just sit around being an economist if nobody will give you a chair to do it in. When you get one, you have to be right on stuff some of the time, particularly if you work for an actual firm like Smith Barney or Merrill Lynch, or else they will blame you when their funds suck wind, as mine have for a really long time and, believe me, I blame them!

The Upside: People think you're brilliant, and you may be!

> All I know is I'm not a Marxist.
>
> **Karl Marx**

The Downside: Your mother leaps off the side of a cruise ship when her retirement account goes south.

The Dark Side: Your ideas are adopted by the ruling class of a third-world nation, who then use them to exterminate the entire middle class.

Where You Go from Here: Bullshit think tank.

36

"Escort"

Give the people what they want

> Discretion is the polite word for hypocrisy.
>
> **Christine Keeler**

$$: If you stay upright, several hundred dollars for the evening; a spanking can go for as much as $1,000 in Framingham, Massachusetts.

ß: 50.

Skills Required: Be of legal age, good company, and be able to fend off advances you don't wish to entertain. Proficiency in Spanish, Bulgarian, Latvian, Chinese, and Japanese may also be helpful.

Duties: Legally, you are being paid for your time and simple companionship, which could include many things and still remain on the right side of the law—including private exotic dancing, role-playing, modeling, sensual massage, all that good kind of stuff.

Famous Examples: Richard Gere as Julian Kaye in *American Gigolo,* who learns six languages while hanging upside down in gravity boots; Julia Roberts as Vivian, Richard Gere's escort in *Pretty Woman*.

> You're a hooker?! Jesus, I thought I was doing great with you!
>
> **Dudley Moore, in *Arthur***

How to Get It: I don't really have to tell you how to get it, do I?

The Upside: Great selection of wigs.

The Downside: You have to tell people that you are a poodle groomer.

The Dark Side: You go to meet one of your clients, and he turns out to be your dad.

Where You Go from Here: Internet entrepreneur.

37

Executive Vice President, New Media

Sell vaporware to space cadets

> Give the people a new word, and they think they have a new fact.
>
> **Willa Cather**

$$: $225,000–$1.5 million per year, with absolutely no ceiling if the firm you are working with turns into a Google of some kind.

ß: 75–150, depending on whether you have the misfortune to get involved in an actual product or service that may, in time, be tested in the real world.

Skills Required: Alert! You're going to need to read. This may go against your bullshit nature, but stick with me. Successful new media people are up on all the current bullshit, including jargon. Things are "sticky" or "platform agnostic," and new forms of technology appear every day that you need to know about, if only to mention them in random conversation to befuddle people. I know a new media guy in my corporation who keeps on about "Blu-ray Disc technology." By the time you read this, that may be a household word, or it may have disappeared into the mists of time along with the eight-track tape player. It doesn't matter. When Bob starts talking Blu-ray, everybody thinks, "Bob is smart." That's what being a new media executive is all about.

Duties: Whip up an enormous storm of bullshit that makes everybody feel like the corporation is on the cutting edge of everything revenue-generating. Lead a team of young, excessively hairy people to find new revenue streams.

Famous Example: The current head of the Aspen Institute, Walter Isaacson. Walter labored long and hard in the Time Warner new media gulag throughout the 1980s and early '90s, trying to keep his corporation on the cusp of all that was interactive, none of which ever materialized for anybody. After that he was rewarded with a bunch of real jobs—editor of *Time* magazine and then president of CNN—neither of which seem ripe with opportunities for indolence. The story has a happy ending, though. Today, Walter is top dog at an educational establishment that caters to the intellectual pretensions of big business. Good luck, Walter! Let me know when I can speak there!

How to Get It: Circulate abstruse articles and treatises on developmental subjects to a lot of folks inside, with a little note on top of the e-mail saying, "This is something we should know about." Organize informal meetings on outlandish subjects in which you bring in guys with shaved heads from Seattle. Clip news stories from arcane publications that imply that your nearest competitors are way ahead of you, the way the Defense Department did about the Russian space program during the cold war. Eventually, you will be given the new media job so that senior management can feel less anxious about the stuff you've made them nervous about.

The Upside: As long as the bubble is full, you're golden. And there's never any need to prove yourself with real results, because people don't want that, they want simply to feel that there's somebody thinking about all of it, and that's you.

The Downside: Hard to see if there is one. Whatever it might be, if you're a really good bullshitter, and I know you are, it will take ten years to discover it.

The Dark Side: Your entrepreneurial friends in this area, who have the courage to push the envelope on the outside of corporate life, are now multitrillionaires. You are slogging along on less than a million a year.

Where You Go from Here: Home, with a massive exit package that finances your next foray into science fiction funded by institutional investors.

38

Expert Witness

Testify what you're paid to

$$: Usually an hourly rate that includes waiting time in court. But the value comes from potential results. For, say, a psychiatrist hired to exonerate an ax murderer, the fee of several thousand dollars per day would not be unthinkable.

ß: 38–93. Certainly, the expert needs a little bit of fact or objective reality on which to base his opinion if, that is, he's not a total whore. If he is, that makes things much easier, and we can settle comfortably on the much higher number.

Churchill: Madam, would you sleep with me for five million pounds?

Socialite: My goodness, Mr. Churchill . . . Well, I suppose . . . we would have to discuss terms, of course . . .

Churchill: Would you sleep with me for five pounds?

Socialite: Mr. Churchill, what kind of woman do you think I am?!

Churchill: Madam, we've already established that. Now we are haggling about the price.

Skills Required: Lower-paid expert witnesses may require nothing more than a degree in psychology or some other squelchy subject. Clearly, experts in arcana like ballistics, toxins, or genetics are much more highly trained.

Duties: Look at evidence in a calm, professional, dispassionate manner, and then testify in such a way as to help the side that is paying you. It's nice when you actually agree with them, by the way. You may digest your food better.

Famous Example: Dr. Michael Baden, a distinguished pathologist and former chief medical examiner of New York City, whose famous cases have included the examination of the remains of Czar Nicholas of Russia and his family, and who testified for the defense in the O. J. Simpson trial, a credential he is careful to include in his résumé.

How to Get It: Advertise. Once you get a buzz going, word of mouth will do the rest.

The Upside: A good, solid living not based on the vagaries of an actual career in your chosen profession.

The Downside: Bad guys get off. Oh well, that's our legal system!

The Dark Side: Bad guy gets off and comes to your house to say thank you.

Where You Go from Here: Reality show psychological consultant.

39

Feng Shui Consultant

Show people how to improve their home, work, and sex life by arranging their physical surroundings in ways that are in harmony with the universe

$$: Cosmic.

> How you do anything is how you do everything.
>
> **Zen proverb**

ß: 72.8. Mostly in the explaining part. How does one convey the movements of the wheels that grind all there is, and how they are expressed in the texture one chooses for one's bedding? And get paid for it, I mean.

Skills Required: Must have a sense of color and line and space, and be knowledgeable about the rules and philosophies that have been established by bullshit artists for millennia.

Duties: Must show up, convey spiritual aura, and immediately help to convince people that your alterations in their physical surroundings are helping them to keep energy flowing. If you find excess yin, move in some yang; conversely, if there is a superfluity of yang, you know what to do with it.

Famous Examples: Huang-shih Kung, of course; Ch'ing Wu; and the editors of *Real Simple.*

How to Get It: Feng shui is an ancient art form based on the Taoist experience of nature, a tradition and discipline shrouded in mystery. This is very good for you, in the sense that both shrouds and mystery are on your side. But unlike business consultancy or closet organization, a true feng shui advisor cannot exist on sheer bullshit alone. There are actual, verifiable traditions and philosophical concepts at work here, and you've got to put in some time to master them unless you're a complete ham hock. Decide whether you are California-style, New Age feng shui, or traditional Chinese. There are many schools—Three Periods, Three Combinations, Mysterious Subtleties, and/or Eight Mansions—all of which have their adherents. The Flying Stars System, for example, can help you assess the flow of invisible energy inside a house. You can train in any one of these systems or cross-train in more than one, if you've got the right shoes. It's probably easier to tout yourself as an artist of traditional Chinese feng shui if you are, in fact, Chinese. But it doesn't really matter. Feng shui is one of the great arts based around that other important Asian attribute: Chutz Pah.

The Upside: You can really make people feel more at home in their surroundings, since the majority of homeowners have very little sense of where to put that credenza.

The Downside: You are called out at 4 a.m. when your No. 1 client feels negative energy coming from her electric blanket.

The Dark Side: There is a distinct possibility that any time now rich people will stop believing in this stuff.

Where You Go from Here: Home Depot, to help people choose the right fixtures!

40

Food Critic

Life is one big doggie bag

How clever are shrimp-and-foie gras dumplings with grapefruit dipping sauce? What if we called them fishy liver-filled condoms. They were properly vile, with a savor that lingered like a lovelorn drunk and tasted as if your mouth had been used as the swab bin in an animal hospital.

A. A. Gill in *Vanity Fair* trashing Jean-Georges Vongerichten's restaurant 66

$$: As God is your witness, you will never go hungry again!

ß: Who knows? These guys eat soaked, marinated, and under-cooked liver and call it foie gras. How much of a food critic's situation is determined by the fact that his taste is exquisitely elevated, and how much is the purveyance of pure snobberyific bullshittery? I mean, come on. They may call it sweetbreads, but it's pancreas, for God's sake!

Skills Required: Eat anything and write about it with wit, aplomb, and a voice accessible to those who might not understand why a burning mound of duck is better than a quietly roasted one, or why a fat-infused chicken breast, once so popular, is now completely out of fashion. Must know more adjectives than just about any other profession, and be handy with metaphors as well. The one hundredth time you have eaten a morsel of beef cheek, you must find a new way to describe it for your readers, lest they think you are just playing it all by the numbers. Was it "a walk in a fragrant pasture, redolent of sunshine and fines herbes"? Or was it "a lusty song of high summer"?

> Only female restaurant critics like sardines.
>
> **Alan Richman, *GQ***

Duties: Wake at noon. Putter around the house. Have a cup of tea. Read the paper. Look at the restaurant reviews and get completely inflamed by professional envy. At about 5:00 p.m., go to the place you're assigned to review, even if you don't really feel like eating kosher-Islamic fusion, with a friend or two or three. Order a ton of food and eat a little bit of everything or a lot. Apply your standards, achieved over years of research, thought, and gourmandizing, to whatever you have plumped into your face.

Famous Examples: French fop and aesthete Brillat-Savarin invented the craft of food writing at the level where the things we eat may be compared to music, painting, and literature. Today, the state of the art resides in such scribes as Ruth Reichl, now editor of *Gourmet* magazine; Alan Richman, who has more James Beard Journalism Awards in his closet than he has pants that fit him; and Jeffrey Steingarten, who can write more amusingly about salt than most people can about sex.

How to Get It: Well, ideally you're supposed to know something about food. People go to schools to learn about seasonings, sauces, techniques of braising and roasting, all that kind of bullshit. But these days, as A. A. Gill has proven, the real fame in this, as in all kinds of current criticism, is the fun people have sharing in your nastiness. The evil that you do will live after you. The good will be interred with your chicken bones.

The Upside: Eat. Drink. Be flabby.

The Downside: Food poisoning. Terminal oenophilia.

The Dark Side: Enraged owner of a restaurant stabs you with a $450 carving knife.

Where You Go from Here: Weight Watchers.

41

Funeral Director

Feast on grief, sell related inventory

> In the long run, we're all dead.
>
> **John Maynard Keynes**

$$: Up to $100,000 per year.

ß: 40—death, my friends, is the ultimate nonbullshit deal. But don't worry. You can still do something with it, as long as it's not yours.

Skills Required: A strong stomach, willingness to drain bodily fluids (not one's own), ownership of a full boxed DVD collection of *Six Feet Under.*

Duties: Sell expensive caskets, catafalques, and associated burial services to people who have just lost a loved one and want their departing rites to be appropriate, meaningful, and reflective of the love and esteem in which they were held. There are no more vulnerable customers. But you have to sell them right. If they get grossed out or feel overtly exploited, they won't be back, a particularly tragic outcome with large families.

> There's tons of legal stuff to learn. There's the Health and Tissue act, different government acts, the Funeral Board act, Funeral Home act. There's a ton of legislation to read. It's pretty dry.
>
> **Future funeral director, HBO Web site**

Famous Example: None. Profile is not part of this particular game.

How to Get It: You must be licensed, at least twenty-one years old, and have studied mortuary science for two to four years, a course of study that includes embalming techniques, restorative art, business management, ethics, and communications. After that, there is a one- to three-year apprenticeship, and part-time jobs are available for aspiring funeral directors in which you learn the basics of the craft, and wash and polish limos and hearses.

The Upside: Wild convention in Vegas.

The Downside: Deep, abiding weirdness, the effect of seeing dead people all day, and not the way the kid in *The Sixth Sense* did, either.

The Dark Side: Reconstructing Sonny Corleone's body after it was shot up on the Cross Bay Bridge.

Where You Go from Here: Stand-up comic.

42

Game Show Host

Smile, read cue cards, sock it away

$$: Just about scale for the little things that appear on the Game Show Network, the ones that make you kind of sad to watch, but huge lifetime stipends for the top players like Vanna White.

> A guy called me smarmy one time. I had to call him up and ask him what it meant.
>
> **Chuck Woolery**

ß: 75. You have to do the same thing year after year after year.

Skills Required: Teeth. Sense of humor. Ability to withstand sense of overwhelming depression brought about by constant contact with very odd people.

Duties: Meet contestant, run game, give away valuable prizes that really and truly, for the most part, have no value. Do it again.

Famous Example(s): Chuck Woolery has been a champ at moving from one sinecure to another, always maintaining the core of what it means to be Chuck Woolery, something indefinable but tangible nonetheless. Allen Ludden was as close to an intellectual as the genre ever produced. Jack Barry with his partner, Dan Enright, fixed the most famous quiz show of their day, *The $64,000 Question*. Groucho Marx, the host of *You Bet Your Life,* succeeded in turning the genre into comedy. And no list would be complete without Wink Martindale.

> **Groucho:** Eight children! Why do you have so many?
>
> **Contestant:** I love my husband, Groucho.
>
> **Groucho:** I love my cigar, but I take it out of my mouth sometimes.
>
> **Groucho Marx to a female contestant, *You Bet Your Life***

How to Get It: See an orthodontist, then an agent.

The Upside: Everybody at the supermarket knows you.

The Downside: You wanted to be something once.

The Dark Side: Existential despair, alcoholism, and descent into obsession about, say, the importance of spaying household pets.

Where You Go from Here: Bit part, Farrelly Brothers movie.

43

Greeter/Cuer

Say hello to people when they come into a store, say hello to people when they come into the store . . .

$$: Minimum wage.

> This store is a bit of a maze. You have to ride three escalators just to buy a toilet brush. That's why we have a cuer at the bottom to guide our customers through. The cuer helps to direct people.
>
> **Store manager, The Home Depot**

ß: 94—absolutely no content whatsoever, but a great opportunity to meet people, if only briefly.

Skills Required: Put on a happy face; remain cool and pleasant to confused and sometimes grumpy customers.

Duties: The greeter, who may sometimes also be what is called a "cuer," is assigned to stand in the doorway of a store, sometimes a large one like Target or a smaller one like Radio Shack, and say hello to the people who enter. If they need directions to a certain department, the greeter must know enough about the establishment to put them on the right path to consumerism.

Famous Example: I was at a Target in California a few months ago. A young man was standing in the doorway, wearing a name tag that said, "Barry." His job was to greet people, and he did that very well. When we were checking out, Barry helped to bag our stuff, even though that was not called for, and then he assisted us in getting the cart, which was laden with all kinds of stupid items you would never have gotten if you hadn't found yourself at Target, out to the car. "You having a good day, Barry?" I asked him. He smiled at me, a huge, disingenuous grin. "Every day is a good day here," he said, as if I were simple. All the way out to the parking lot, Barry talked about how much he loved Target, how the store had allowed him to keep his benefits when he moved from another locale, how nice everybody—fellow employees and customers—were. When he was done loading the trunk with me, I gave him five bucks for his trouble. He looked at it, confused, and then waved it away, almost insulted. I felt bad. For this guy, the job was reward enough. Here, then, was living proof that there is happiness in any bullshit job, if it is the right one for you.

How to Get It: Apply.

The Upside: Easy to learn the drill.

The Downside: Sometimes your face hurts.

The Dark Side: Your college buddy shows up with the girl you used to go out with.

Where You Go from Here: Bathroom attendant who provides full-service hand wash, mouthwash, and complimentary scent.

Guru

Explain meaning of the universe to people who require it

> Some people, well, if they don't like Scientology, well, then, fuck you. Really. Fuck you. Period.
>
> **Tom Cruise, *Rolling Stone*, August 11, 2004**

$$: There's big money in guru status. Obviously, a guru like Tom Cruise doesn't need the money, but the organization that he represents, just like all that sell a certain kind of spiritual solution to their adherents, do very well fleecing their flock in a variety of ways. Scientology charges members huge sums of money—tens of thousands of dollars a pop—to continue their spiritual training. Those who can't pay, and most can't, work off their debt to the church by proselytizing for it. Hence the legions of poor droids in the street asking if you'd like to take some free personality testing. But this is relatively mild compared with the price that the Reverend Jim Jones exacted from his congregation at Jonestown, Guyana, or that the Reverend Sun Myung Moon imposes on his weird congregants.

ß: 110. The thing that separates the guru from the run-of-the-mill cleric is that the guru presents himself as a personal incarnation of something or other, and himself becomes the object of worship. Needless to say, this can often be highly advantageous for the guru. Throughout the 1960s and '70s, a whole bunch of Western dudes transformed themselves into one kind of Rinpoche or Ram Dass or other and immediately attracted Manson-style harems to themselves, in which the will of the cosmos was manifested most satisfyingly, often several times a day.

> The whole world is in my hands, and I will conquer and subjugate the whole world.
>
> **Rev. Sun Myung-Moon**

Skills Required: Must have deep, penetrating gaze. Be able to reel in disassociated, needy people, take their money, dismantle their egos, and reassemble them for your own purposes.

Duties: To be is to do. To do is to be. Do be do be do.

Famous Examples: There are many, beginning with the genuine avatars who started all the world's major religions, from Moses to Jesus to Mohammed to Buddha to Mary Baker Eddy. There was something very special about them all, in that they were all sincere, rich with ideas and understanding, and not strictly in it for the conquest of souls.

Somewhere along the line it must have gotten easier to get the job.

How to Get It: You may have to move to northern California if you want to make it easy on yourself, but if you're an incipient Nazi, there's plenty of room for growth in this bullshit business in Idaho, Montana, and the Midwest.

The Upside: No matter how full of bullshit you are, nobody calls you on it. If you're very good, you may sop up all the goods and chattels of a surprising number of people, and have more wives than is legal.

The Downside: Hard to find a good place to put all that money.

The Dark Side: It's not easy being a sociopath.

Where You Go from Here: Direct sales.

45

Handler

Pave the way for the rich and pesky

$$: $125,000.

ß: 56–185.

Skills Required: The handler must be a problem solver. Problems are often solved before they happen, so the handler must also be a great planner and anticipator. After the hotel room has been trashed or the cocaine has been discovered at the airport security checkpoint, the handler needs to be a great negotiator and wheedler. Since the handler will be blamed for any problem created by he or she who needs the handling, the handler must also be strong, persuasive, and able to kick ass and take names. In short, a tough, tough job, suitable only for those who

> I've done it their way and now it's my turn. I'm my own handler. Any questions? Ask me . . . there's not going to be any more handler stories because I'm the handler.
>
> **Dan Quayle, responding to press reports of his staff having to, in effect, potty train him**

can put up with a lot of bullshit from big bullshit artists, and at times give as good as they get.

Duties: Help the itty-bitty baby if he or she is about to get into twubble.

Famous Examples: The third Scientologist from the right who travels with Katie Holmes; the team of gray men that arrives before the president is to speak at the Hilton to check that there is bottled water; Renfield, the ghoul who traveled with Dracula, making sure there was a juicy virgin to munch on and a safe place for his coffin every night.

How to Get It: The handler is usually the pointy nose of a large organization that serves what is known as "talent" in a wide variety of ways. "Talent" is a very inclusive word. There are many senior executives of corporations who are considered talent. Actors, of course, are talent, but so are fashion designers, rock stars, and celebrity cardiologists. Anyone who performs a semi-nonfungible role in our society and has the right to scream, "Do You Know Who I Am!?" is talent. The handler handles all of that. It's a dangerous job and built for those who like to travel solo, live close to the edge, and carry a big stick that belongs to somebody else.

The Upside: Proximity to large dudes.

The Downside: You can't yell back.

The Dark Side: Cleaning up dog puke at 4 a.m. in a Vegas parking lot, because Phideaux had a bad ride on the G4.

Where You Go from Here: Tour manager, Rolling Stones Iron Lung Good-bye Tour.

46

Handwriting Analyst

Profile human behavior. Interpret meaningless chicken scratches without laughing.

$$: A good handwriting analyst can make $100 per hour at a cocktail party; big ones who are asked to authenticate major documents are very well paid, particularly since they rarely are capable of being definitive and mostly offer a raft of bullshit rationalizations and excuses for not being more certain of anything.

ß: 126.

Skills Required: Must know a bunch of pseudo-objective measurements and signifiers by

> **HAMLET**
> Do you see yonder cloud that's almost in shape of a camel?
>
> **LORD POLONIUS**
> By the mass, and 'tis like a camel, indeed . . .
>
> **HAMLET**
> Or like a whale?
>
> **LORD POLONIUS**
> Very like a whale.
>
> **HAMLET**
> Then I will come to my mother by and by.
>
> ***Hamlet,* Act 3, Scene 2**

which people's handwriting is reflective of their character.

Duties: Look at handwriting of subject, make stuff up. Authenticate signatures on important documents, within, you know, a certain range of certitude, unless it's from a photocopier, or the sun is in your eyes, or the paper got wet, or the bat was too heavy, or your head hurts.

Famous Examples: Five European doctors whose names are important only to their descendents did most of the research that founded this discipline in the middle of the last century, working independently from Russia, Germany, England, and Hungary at around the same time that a bunch of wacky sciences were being established. Today, this bullshit is very valuable in legal settings where confusing juries is of primary importance, and a variety of approaches—from holistic graphology to symbolic analysis—are available for you to sling around.

How to Get It: The good news is that correspondence schools seem to be the way to go, leaving you free to do other bullshit while you're grinding away at your new profession. Best of all, since there is very little agreement among graphologists about the meaning of anything, you can develop your own approach pretty much at will once you have that hard-won sheepskin. Happy bullshitting!

The Upside: Great glow of science about a whole bunch of mumbo jumbo. Get to hang with other graphologists, who are really fun at parties.

The Downside: Clients get very annoyed when they rely on you to authenticate things and all you can give them is a raft of halting excuses and mumbling horseshit.

The Dark Side: Sudden conviction that life is meaningless and the truth is essentially unknowable.

Where You Go from Here: Water dowser.

47

Headhunter

Put big jobs together with big people, at about the rate at which an elephant gestates

$$: $250,000 a year and up.

ß: 160. Huge. Almost Trumpian levels. The catch-22 is that you can't get taken seriously by a headhunter unless you have a great job, and you can't get that great job unless you have the attentions of a headhunter. This works well for only one entity in the transaction: the headhunter.

Skills Required: Truly, I don't know. It's hard to figure.

Duties: Try to find a perfect person to fill that very impor-

> Sure, I can ground Orr. But first he has to ask me to."
>
> "That's all he has to do to be grounded?"
>
> "That's all. Let him ask me."
>
> "And then you can ground him?" Yossarian asked.
>
> "No. Then I can't ground him."
>
> "You mean there's a catch?"
>
> "Sure there's a catch," Doc Daneeka replied. "Catch 22. Anyone who wants to get out of combat duty isn't really crazy."
>
> **Joseph Heller, *Catch-22***

tant slot at a company that really needs one. Finding the person is not required. Your role is to provide the illusion of activity for the senior officer who hired you, so that when the chairman says, "Do we have an EVP of finance yet?" your client can say, "Not yet, Howie, but we have Shinem and Grubb working on it!"

Famous Example: The Asmat tribe of New Guinea, who reputedly killed and ate Michael Rockefeller, the twenty-three-year-old son of then New York Governor Nelson Rockefeller.

How to Get It: Background in human resources is very helpful because it trains you to stop caring about people. The trick is to get fired from the HR department of a large company. Headhunting firms seem to be filled with losers from the corporate wars.

The Upside: Big, formerly successful people come to you on their knees, begging for a lift back onto the gravy train.

The Downside: You're a human resources professional.

The Dark Side: Sitting with people who really need you, and you know you can't help them. That bothers even you at times, admit it.

Where You Go from Here: Military recruiter for the Iraqi army.

48

HMO Health Care Professional

See sick people, get rid of them

$$: Not so great, actually. You could do a lot better as a plastic surgeon, allergist (see Allergist), or any specialist not supported by insurance.

> They would rather see me doubles over in pain greater than labor than fix the problems, not even attmepting to prescribe pain meds nothing. Kaiser is the biggest pile of bullshit ever invented.
>
> **Beth, a patient, writing on kaiserhospitalsucks.com, one of many sites dedicated to complaints about just one of many HMOs**

ß: 45–121. The number is potentially reduced by the damage you are sometimes forced to do by the HMO's policies of stalling, delay, and steadfast inattention to those in need.

Skills Required: Be elusive. Be able to make patients come back again and again, generating multiple bills for no service received; prescribe wrong medication at times; pooh-pooh ailments of chronic sufferers.

Duties: Your job is to see as many people as possible and recommend the least expensive treatment you can. Least expensive for the HMO, that is. A young friend of mine had chronic neck pain a while back in the early days of managed care. The Harvard Community Health Plan gave him a prescription for Darvon and a neck collar and sent him home—four times. He's all right now. He saw a private physician who gave him some simple CAT scans, found the problem, and removed a tumor the size of a grapefruit from his spine. It only took six months in a body cast and metal halo to set him right, but he had already moved from Boston when he was hospitalized, so it didn't cost his HMO a thing, so in the end it was a happy story.

Famous Examples: There really are no big names in undercaring for people. I recommend you simply enter the words "HMO horror stories" in Google and see what pops up. It is a lesson in how dangerous bullshit can be when it is placed in the wrong hands.

How to Get It: You may have to earn your MD to undertreat people at the highest levels of this job. But a great HMO has callous and deliberately inattentive people at all levels—from the receptionist who keeps you waiting in the wrong area despite knowing that you're not in the right place, to the scheduling nurse who puts you on hold and then forgets about you, to the specialist who could ease your suffering but sends you to another department for further testing because he'd rather not. At the very tippity top of the food chain here are administrators adept in doling out huge portions of bullshit to people in order to explain why the HMO has decided not to treat their terminal disease. You can be that person, as long as you're not afraid that one day your karma will give you a goiter.

The Upside: After a while, figuring out ways to deny people medical attention can be a challenging game. The good news is that you win more than you lose.

The Downside: Sometimes people get so sick that you may have to treat them.

The Dark Side: Even though it's not really your fault and you're only enforcing the codes and regulations of the system you work for, and everybody has to make a living, you know, sometimes it's very narrowly possible that you may do something, or not do something, that results in the death of somebody. Then, you know, if you think about it too much and dwell on it in a way that you really have no reason to, you may feel bad.

Where You Go from Here: Hunting endangered species for their fur.

49

Human Billboard

Sell body space to interested morons

$$: In 2005, the inventor of this new profession, Andrew Fischer of Nebraska, sold his forehead on eBay to SnoreStop for $37,375 for one month.

> As I go around town doing my thing—your domain name will be plastered smack dab cross my noggin.
>
> **Andrew Fischer**

ß: 50. Finding a new way to merchandise something that people always thought was a noncommercial property isn't bullshit, Sparky.

Skills Required: Must know how to sell something on eBay. That's a skill in itself, you know. I tried to sell a very nice coffee table book there once, and you know how many bids I got for it?

Duties: Have forehead. Investigate line extensions to other body parts.

Famous Example(s): Andrew Fischer began it, but if one is interested in selling virtually any body part, there is now a place to do it. Body Billboardz, for instance, is described as "a network bringing together those who are willing to sell space on their body with advertisers interested in buying that space." Included are venues on arm, back, chest, head, leg, and other. I'm interested in other.

How to Get It: Have a body with enough hairless, clear space on it to accommodate messages of varying length.

The Upside: That big butt of yours is finally worth something.

The Downside: Some social acquaintances may find you crass.

The Dark Side: The part of your brain stem that was intended to accomplish anything with your life atrophies, and you are left with nothing but a tiny nub useful only for subsequent crackpot schemes.

Where You Go from Here: Politics.

50

Industrial Psychologist

Utilize principles of behavioral psychology at the behest of senior management to manipulate minds of unsuspecting employees

$$: Corporate salary—not the top but not the bottom, either. If you can wrangle the gig into an executive vice president position in human resources, low seven figures is not impossible since you control compensation.

> Management must smother individualism in the workplace. Any employee who refuses to sacrifice everything for "the company" should be fired.
>
> **W. Edwards Deming, father of the post-WWII industrial revolution in Japan and one of the great avatars of the quality revolution**

ß: 62. There's a little something in psychology, you know. It's putting it to the use of the corporation that's bullshit.

Skills Required: A PhD if you're not going to be thought a total fraud. On the other hand, forget it.

Duties: Diddle with people's heads so they become more productive and docile.

Famous Examples: Frank Gilbreth, the original dad in *Cheaper by the Dozen,* was the first to use behaviorial psychology to manipulate workers. Since then, there have been many, most notably Tom Peters, who sold Excellence to an entire generation of mediocre business executives.

How to Get It: There are quite a few online and off-brand educational institutions that offer a degree in industrial or organizational psychology. For some reason, a fair number of the more elevated establishments seem not to.

The Upside: Able to turn perfectly serviceable workers into drooling zombies.

The Downside: You turn into a skinny, tweedy old fart with hair everywhere but on your head.

The Dark Side: You are in league with the devil. This is not all bad, of course. That side eats more meat and less fish than the good guys.

Where You Go from Here: Torture lab rats in research experiments to develop better eyedrops.

51

Infomercial Spokesperson/ Celebrity Pitchman

Lend personal imprimatur to sell crap in paid programming time

> They've been looking for that fountain of youth in a jar, and it's actually going to come in a mask!
>
> **Linda Evans, selling the Rejuvenique mask, powered by a 9-volt battery, which tightens up facial muscles by injecting electric current into them**

$$: Millions! Billions! Hundreds of thousands sold! Not available in any store!

ß: 198, but only to save two points for Donald Trump.

Skills Required: Shameless pitchmanship, ability to hawk benefits of products that might become centerpiece of stand-up comedy routine; prior career as a B-level actor desirable.

Duties: Market products that nobody in the world would ever think worthy of producing to a huge, mass audience.

> It helps me maintain my sexy, you feel me?
>
> **Sean "Puffy" Combs, aka P. Diddy, Puff Daddy, and Diddy, advertising Proactiv Solution acne treatment in an infomercial that paid him $3 million for a four-hour shoot**

Famous Examples: One master inventor and marketer stands tall above all. Ron Popeil, inventor of a bewildering array of products that are sold in thirty-minute infomercials that for some reason, like a car accident, are impossible to pull one's eyes away from. Products invented by Ron Popeil's Ronco company include the Showtime Standard Rotisserie and the Professional Rotisserie, each of which cooks a chicken while sealing in all of its juices. The collection of Six Star Cutlery (a descendant of the famous Ginsu knife set); the 5-Tray Electric Food Dehydrator; the Solid Flavor Injector, which "seasons food inside and out"; the Popeil's Pasta Maker; the famous Popeil Pocket Fisherman; the GLH Formula 9 Hair System, which eliminates bald spots by spraying on fake "hair"; the Inside-The-Shell Egg Scrambler, which scrambles an egg *right in the shell;* the Bagel Cutter; the Dial-O-Matic, which slices and dices vegetables into more pieces than the former Yugoslavia; the Flip-Its, which just might replace traditional barbecue tongs, forks, and spatulas!; and the Door Saver, which protects your car from garage walls and other cars, and has something to do with tassels.

How to Get It: There are two tiers in this line. The first is the fading celebrity who lends his or her tiny glow to the proceedings. But there is generally a second banana, tasting and exclaiming and going all googly-eyed about the benefits of the gizmo, paste, or regimen. You can be that, if you read the show business trade magazines and look for auditions for the jobs. You don't have to be talented. In fact, judging from the quality of the infomercials themselves, it would help not to be.

> I'm thrilled to be helping spread the message that people can live more and get more from their daily lives by using T-Mobile's service just as I do.
>
> **Catherine Zeta-Jones**

The Upside: Free stuff, big money, unless you're the nodding dummy tasting the perfectly grilled chicken, then my guess is all you're getting is scale plus perfectly grilled chicken.

The Downside: Terminal loss of self-respect.

The Dark Side: Electric antiwrinkle mask gets wet and sears your face off.

Where You Go from Here: North Korean brainwashing academy.

52

Insurance Broker

Bore and frighten people into purchasing insurance

> There are worse things in life than death. Have you ever spent an evening with an insurance salesman?
>
> **Woody Allen**

$$: Between $25,000 for the least successful to about $125,000 for the crème de la crop. Brilliant insurance salesmen can earn more because their pay is based on commissions, some solely on them, which. explains why once an insurance broker gets ahold of you he doesn't let go until he's shaken your spleen out of you.

ß: 119. The actual need to close sales depresses this number.

Skills Required: I want you to read the following paragraph from the U.S. Department of Labor's Bureau of Labor Statistics:

> As the demand for financial products and financial planning increases, many insurance agents are choosing to gain the proper licensing and certification to sell securities and other financial products. Doing so, however, requires substantial study and passing an additional examination—either the Series 6 or Series 7 licensing exam, both of which are administered by the National Association of Securities Dealers (NASD). The Series 6 exam is for individuals who wish to sell only mutual funds and variable annuities, whereas the Series 7 exam is the main NASD series license that qualifies agents as general securities sales representatives. In addition, to further demonstrate competency in the area of financial planning, many agents find it worthwhile to earn the certified financial planner or chartered financial consultant designation.

If you can't read it without falling asleep or going to get a sandwich in the middle of it, you can't be an insurance broker.

Duties: Deal with matters of soul-destroying tedium (and, in the case of health and life insurance, some psychic discomfort), and enthusiastically sell them to people. The good part, at least in my experience, is that once you've brokered the sale of automobile, life, whatever, your job is done, babe.

Famous Examples: Insurance as a business, as opposed to a means of extortion as practiced by the Romans (and their descendants in the mob), was invented in England in the late 1500s, as London entrepreneurs made their way around a city that was clearly ready to go up in flames, and down to docks laden with ships whose potential sinking would no doubt ruin their wealthy owners. Sure enough, in 1666, there was a huge fire in London, and after that you really couldn't get around without a lot of insurance. Today, a true plethora of insurance options are available and even mandatory for the average bourgeois citizen: health insurance that guarantees a minimum of care—literally; life insurance that usually lapses right when you do; automobile insurance that is relatively reasonable unless you use it; home owner's insurance; and many other interesting types of insurance that usually one spouse in a couple is obsessed with, leading to divorce.

How to Get It: You do need to be licensed, I think. I'm not clear about that. I read the pertinent information about it but can't seem to retain it. It's a regulated industry, whatever that's worth these days, so you probably need to pass something to get bonded or certified or both. Good luck.

The Upside: Steady, nonthreatening if unexciting employment for someone who likes to leave his job at the office.

The Downside: People glaze over and back away, having suddenly remembered a prior appointment, almost as dramatically as they would if you told them you were a mortician.

The Dark Side: You wake up one morning and realize that you radiate boringness the way some people throw off body odor.

Where You Go from Here: Classic rock disc jockey.

53

Investment Banker

Strumpet of capital

$$: Boooooo-yah!

> A bank is a place that will lend you money if you can prove you don't need it.
>
> **Bob Hope**

ß: 123. Although it's on the way up, definitely. A great potential investment!

Skills Required: Market ice to Eskimos.

Duties: Make enormous fees by selling corporations on the benefits of consolidation and acquisition; then make huge subsequent fees by turning around and convincing the very same corporations to deconsolidate and divest noncore assets; attend conferences where rumors can be circulated and companies put into play. Trade the enterprises that provide the lifeblood of millions of workers like plastic chips in a cheap card game.

Famous Examples: I really don't want to say. I may want to fund a start-up business one day.

How to Get It: Must attend many conferences and hang with financial types, bullshitting extensively about ways perfectly good businesses can be blown up, macerated, pureed, or jammed together with others for no particular reason other than that nobody has done it yet. If you look at really stupid deals and do not say "why," but instead say "why not," then you've got what it takes.

The Upside: These guys are so rich their Bentleys have Bentleys.

The Downside: Sometimes you get a hangnail getting out of the limo.

The Dark Side: You must consort with many, many moguls. Every occupation has its tools, but they're really big ones.

Where You Go from Here: In ten or fifteen years, *you* could be a mogul, with your own investment bankers hanging off you like remoras.

54

Lawyer

Manipulate the legal system for the benefit of oneself and one's clients

> Make crime pay. Become a lawyer.
>
> **Will Rogers**

$$: The more odious you are, the bigger the payday.

ß: 33. You have to know an annoying amount of stuff to be a lawyer, so the amount of pure bullshit can be relatively low. The quality is high, though.

Skills Required: Maintain any position someone will pay you for.

Duties: Win.

Famous Examples: Too numerous to mention. There are lawyers in the Bible, for goodness' sake. In our time, the most successful lawyers are those who can get a patently guilty person off. It isn't just the high-octane guys who infuse our culture, though, it's also the tax lawyers and divorce lawyers, God help us, and the corporate lawyers and lawyers who sue people for a living, and those who do nothing but trusts and wills, and a bunch who defend Mafiosi and drug dealers, who do very well in the press. There are so many famous lawyers you can't even name them all. So let's not.

> The first thing we do, let's kill all the lawyers.
>
> Shakespeare, *Henry VI, Part II*

How to Get It: Even worse than becoming a doctor. Reading and reading and reading and memorizing and spouting back law after statute after federal regulatory policy. Ugh. It takes several years, and you have to study all kinds of law, even if you're only interested in one. You also have to be indoctrinated into the core belief that makes it possible for lawyers to live with themselves: that all sides in a disagreement have the right to the best possible counsel. Like any powerful weapon, however, it is dangerous when it falls into the wrong hands. Guys that are too short, for instance, and wear suspenders. Chucklicious, greasy weasels who pride themselves on the size of their multimillion dollar settlements. Sleazy earwigs who crawl into the auditory canal of the media and lay eggs there. And what of all the fine lawyers who occupy our Congress!

The Upside: Lawyers who love it are the happiest campers in the world.

The Downside: For every happy lawyer there are 10,000 miserable bastards with big fat briefcases surgically attached to their arms.

The Dark Side: You feel good when you do bad things.

Where You Go from Here: Court TV.

55

Life Coach

Take over hapless people's entire existence and reshape it in ways that you think are good for them

$$: Successful practitioners in this relatively new field can earn as much as a psychiatrist—hundreds of dollars an hour. But unburdened by the same ethical constraints, an aggressive bullshit artist could conceivably view his or her compensation as a percentage of the life that is being fully, you know, actualized.

> You put your whole
> self in,
> You put your whole
> self out;
> You put your whole
> self in,
> And you shake it all
> about.
> You do the Hokey-Pokey,
> And you turn yourself
> around.
> That's what it's all about.
>
> **Anonymous**

ß: 86–154.

Skills Required: Boss people around in the name of therapy.

Duties: There will always be room for people who want to "help" others by seizing control of them. The life coach is perhaps one of the most fascinating because he or she takes literally the entire existence of his customer under his wing. Think of the power and the responsibility! Thank goodness you're up to it, huh?

Famous Example: Dr. Phil.

How to Get It: You can either join a company that coaches the life out of people, or do it on your own. It doesn't matter. The pay is probably better on your own, if you can hack it. But the benefits are likely to be superior if you work for a life coaching corporation of some kind.

The Upside: It feels good when people pay you to yell at them.

The Downside: Some days you may not be positive enough to get out there and make people bark that happy song.

The Dark Side: Every now and then you see one of your success stories sucking the pavement in front of your local tavern.

Where You Go from Here: High school hockey coach.

56

Mail Order/Online Minister

Help people get married, do baptisms and funerals, and perform other popular, lucrative functions after minimal online ordination

> We believe only in that which is right, and everyone has the right to determine what is right for themselves.
>
> **Rev. Kirby Hensley, Universal Life Church, Modesto, California**

$$: Whatever people are willing to pay, and if you're willing to dress up as Elvis, Moses, or Marilyn (Manson or Monroe). KA-CHING!

ß: 100–154.

Skills Required: None. Dogs, dead persons, and death row inmates have been legally ordained in this manner.

Duties: Weddings, funerals, basically every religious ceremony but bar mitzvahs (although some Reform congregations are willing to talk).

Famous Examples: The Reverend Kirby Hensley, top dog at the Universal Life Church, which he founded in

1959, ordained the Beatles, George Burns, Merle Haggard, and other famous sinners, and successfully defended his nonprofit tax status many times.

How to Get It: To be ordained in the Universal Life Church, log onto the church's Web site, register your name in their database, offer a small "donation." That's it. Congratulations. You're a minister in the church.

The Upside: Even instant ministers are entitled to many discounts, plus parking spaces near nursing homes and prisons.

The Downside: Some states will require you to register, and you can't marry people in certain areas of Virginia or New York City.

The Dark Side: If there is a hell, you're going there. Of course, so are the rest of us.

Where You Go from Here: Online plastic surgeon.

57

Marriage Counselor

Help people complete the destruction of their marriage

> I'm still friends with all my exes—apart from my husbands.
>
> **Cher**

$$: Some charge on a sliding scale, depending on the income of the suffering couple. While some marriage counselors may be MD psychiatrists or PhD psychologists, a fair amount simply have degrees in social work or counseling, and they get paid okay, too.

ß: 65. This is a different kind of bullshit from a lot of the categories we've been studying. This is sad bullshit, dark and full of curdled hope. Too often, the counseling is based on the principle that if a couple talks out its differences, it will help them solve the issues that are driving them apart. That's the bullshit part.

Skills Required: Keep a clean office. Have a degree in something, if you can.

Duties: Listening. Bullshit therapists will try to "cure" the problem. The really good ones will simply sit and allow the waves of anger, guilt, and resentment to wash over them like surf at high tide. Hey, it beats heroin.

> A sweetheart is a bottle of wine. A wife is a wine bottle.
>
> **Baudelaire**

Famous Examples: Did you ever know a couple who went to marriage therapy that is not now divorced? Maybe you do. Maybe you're one of them. Good for you! I mean it!

How to Get It: You can go the social service agency route, but they may want you to have a master's degree of some sort. You may be too much of a bullshitter for that, huh? Tell you what. Go to a Home Depot. Purchase a shingle. Hang it outside your door.

The Upside: You're single!

The Downside: It's like working in a coal mine in which the canary keels over and dies every day.

The Dark Side: You get a large dog and move into a small houseboat on the marina.

Where You Go from Here: Bartender.

58

McKinsey Hit Man

Advise senior management how to keep bonuses by cutting overhead; act as pod person, replacing middle management with other McKinseyites

> You may not be interested in strategy, but strategy is interested in you.
>
> **Leon Trotsky**

$$: Starts very nice, goes up to gazillions.

ß: 190. Bullshit with PowerPoint.

Skills Required: Must be able to make other people feel stupid, and have enormous command of contemporary business jargon, drilling deep for impactful upside. Note: a McKinsey consultant cannot be fat. Tall and skinny, if you can cut that, but at least fit. And if you're losing your hair, shave it all off to create a classic bullethead.

Duties: Go in. Fire the weakest. Aim at a few strong middle managers who may challenge you later. Take them out.

Move into the office next to the CEO. When he's not looking, push him out the window.

Famous Example: James O. McKinsey, an accounting professor at the University of Chicago, who in 1926 set up shop in the Windy City as one of the first management consultants. Today, companies spend some $100 billion on consultants worldwide.

How to Get It: An MBA has a certain shine, a crispness and distance from the rest of humanity. This makes you a pretty lousy blues musician, doctor, or novelist, but it makes you a great player in this end of the game.

The Upside: License to kill comes with the job.

The Downside: People run away and hide in the AV closet when they see you coming.

The Dark Side: You are found with a chicken skewer through your neck at the company retreat in Boca.

Where You Go from Here: Editor, *Harvard Business Review.*

59

Media Trainer

Turn Crows into Songbirds

You . . . look . . . marvelous!

Billy Crystal

$$: $250,000 and up.

ß: 75–160, depending on the businessperson you have been hired to train.

Skills Required: Media management is a very discreet form of bullshit manipulation, and it takes a pro to teach it to people who are generally as bad at taking management as they are at giving it, and who are often ugly, which in real life isn't a problem for the most part, but on camera may present additional challenges.

Duties: Teach shy, buffuddled introverts how to make love to the camera.

Famous Example: When I was a young man working at a now-dead corporation, I had the opportunity to work with some very woolly, unpolished senior management who, while quite lovable at times, were completely untutored and incapable when it came to dealing with the media. To help them, we called the Yoda of such things, a guy named Chester Burger, who had trained under Metternich. Chet spent the day with about six of our guys. By the time they departed from the makeshift TV studio we had set up in our conference room, each felt taller, more handsome or beautiful, and more in control. They were missing only one thing they had originally brought with them: their fear of the camera. They were rarin' to go!

How to Get It: News stories are constructed in a very specific way, and your guys must understand the role that their interface will play in it. Eventually, they will achieve mastery. The good news is that to some extent they will always need you. This bullshit is *not* like riding a bike. It's new and perilous every single time. So you can plan on a monthly retainer.

The Upside: The satisfaction that comes from preparing the innocent and defenseless to do battle with Evil.

The Downside: Much of the clay you work with is either too runny or too hard.

The Dark Side: Sitting at home with a beer one night, you see the politician you adroitly trained explain with perfect pitch why the Katrina relief effort was going so well.

Where You Go from Here: See Dolphin Trainer.

60

Meteorologist on TV

Look good, play with map

> You don't need a weatherman to know which way the wind blows.
>
> **Bob Dylan**

$$: Local weathermen make in the low six figures; those on national morning television can earn millions and reap commercial benefits as well.

ß: 120; could be higher, but there is an occasional tsunami or devastating natural event in which some nonbullshit expertise and credibility is required.

Skills Required: Show up. Dress well. Must be able to transition from total horseshit chitchat to deliver information of some import to those who need to know how to dress that day, then merge back into empty geniality.

Note: This bullshit job is not to be confused with work in the actual field of weather forecasting and meteorology! If you are interested in pursuit of a bullshit profession, that is not the way to go. True meteorologists work for the military, the National Weather Service, and for a host of businesses whose operations depend on accurate forecasting of natural events and disasters. Stick to what you do well!

> A hard rain's a-gonna fall.
>
> **Bob Dylan**

Duties: Be able to talk while standing up and gesturing behind oneself to a blank wall that through technological sleight of hand appears to be a map to those watching the television.

Famous Examples: My personal favorite was Tex Antoine, who worked on WABC in New York. Antoine began his career as a character called Uncle Weatherbee. Before the days of three-dimensional computer-generated art, this charismatic, urbane professional broadcaster and meteorologist would literally draw the local and national weather systems he was talking about on big sheets of blank paper mounted on an easel next to him, describing where the weather systems had been, their likely path, and the implications for the next day's weather. He was great. But one night in the 1970s, Tex's segment followed a gruesome rape story, perhaps an infelicitous setup for the weather forecast, but there you have it. At any rate, the jaunty and perpetually naughty weatherman paused before his forecast with the look of somebody about to deliver a clever riposte, and you could almost see the train bearing down on him in slow motion. He then uttered the career-killing words, "Remember what Confucius said: in case of rape, sit back and enjoy it." The anchors winced. The next night, he was gone.

How to Get It: Be the guy with the best hair and no interest in actual news per se. Develop a schtick that is all your own. I can't tell you what that is, but the great ones all have them. Kiss babies. Tell gags. Lose 150 pounds. Have a pet weasel. The good news is that the weather, believe it or not, is the most important single element in any local or national morning newscast. If you do well, you're set for life.

The Upside: Opportunity to scare people when an inch of snow is coming.

The Downside: People actually blame you for bad weather.

The Dark Side: When a true natural disaster pops up, they send Anderson Cooper!

Where You Go from Here: Sidekick in an infomercial with Emeril.

61

Mogul

Make tons of money for self/others, foam at mouth, be envied and despised

> If I only had a little humility, I'd be perfect.
>
> **Ted Turner**

$$: You can't even talk about it unless you blew past a billion in assets and several hundred million a year a long time ago.

ß: 49–199. You're a hard-working monster who churns out productive activity that lights cities and constructs civilizations. When you bark, the world sits up and begs.

Skills Required: Dominate any room in which you find yourself, control every conversation, intimidate those who terrify others, tower over those who loom over their own landscapes, scare the scary, make silent those who never shut up, go where you want to go, do who you want to do, be always and relentlessly nothing but yourself.

Duties: Build empires. Maintain altitude and attitude. It's not enough to manage existing structures. You've got to see a couple of billboards and envision an entire new way of delivering programming to people and people to advertisers, as Ted Turner did when he inherited his father's dinky little outdoor advertising business.

> Definitely, it's a fear of failure that drives me.
>
> **Jerry Bruckheimer**

Famous Examples: There have been so many moguls throughout the march of time. It's fun to think about all of them, striding about, killing people, defining their cultures by the size and overpowering scent of their personalities. Here are just a few who erected worlds and defined the management culture of their civilizations:

- Xerxes, king of Persia: Cool beard, sweet quality of life for senior management.
- Julius Caesar of Rome: Intellectual man of action whose management of his executive team left something to be desired.
- Attila the Hun: Excellent senior officer with bad PR.
- Genghis Khan: Great acquisition machine, not so good at producing subsequent value.
- Elizabeth I of England: Tough, smelly woman who still garnered the love and respect of her entire empire.
- Otto von Bismarck: Built Germany, for what that's worth.

• Rupert Murdoch: What a guy. Owns the company that publishes me. Everybody loves him.

How to Get It: Go out and take it! Walk with big shoes! Kill the enemy! Reward your friends prodigiously! Eat with the sharks! But lightly!

The Upside: You are the shit. This is an expression used by younger people to denote the highest form of regard for a person's size and power. It used to be "da bomb," but now it's "the shit." You're it.

The Downside: Your best work was done a decade ago, and all that's left is the fear you inspire in others.

The Dark Side: You can't form any personal attachments and are always miserable. Moguls are generally living proof that money cannot buy happiness, which is probably one of their best qualities.

Where You Go from Here: The Herb Allen conference in Sun Valley, Idaho, where you get to consort with other moguls of various stripes and sizes, talk about destructive deals, and feel generally uncomfortable pretending to relax.

62

Mogul/Rock Star/ Celebrity's Ex

Party on!

$$: $250 million. I'm just picking a number.

> I'm a marvelous housekeeper. Every time I leave a man, I keep his house.
>
> **Zsa Zsa Gabor**

ß: 180.

Skills Required: Be tough, spend money. Generate occasional publicity for own activities, be they charitable or uncharitable; must have long legs, high cheekbones, big blond hair that gets increasingly blond as years go by, and a huge accent, either Eastern European or Texan.

Duties: Get plastic surgery as required, acquire "royal" boyfriend from small European nation, write a roman à clef as therapy, appear in fabulous locations in garb given to you by aspiring designers, purchase well-known jewelry and then sell it on QVC, make your divorce lawyer famous by publicizing the size of the deal he got you.

> How many husbands have I had? You mean apart from my own?
>
> **Zsa Zsa Gabor**

Famous Examples: Jerry Hall, Mick Jagger's most recent ex, who says, "I think if I weren't so beautiful, maybe I'd have more character."

How to Get It: Many very wealthy, narcissistic men are incapable of remaining in love for more than a few years. That's good news for those shopping in that market.

The Upside: Perpetual wealth and notoriety.

The Downside: Continual cosmetic surgery.

The Dark Side: Your Italian count might be using you.

Where You Go from Here: Appearing as Mrs. Robinson in the road show of *The Graduate*.

> We were both in love with him. I fell out of love with him, but he didn't.
>
> **Zsa Zsa Gabor**

63

Motivational Speaker

Fill people with hope for five minutes

$$: Quadrillions. But remember. Success without fulfillment is failure. That's why we have such a good fulfillment center.

ß: Immeasurable, because in the great exemplars the bullshit is so artfully mingled and intertwined with actual received wisdom that its essential nature is deracinated and pasteurized.

> It's the integration of those human experiences and the understanding of the psychology of human needs that allows us to bring you the best technologies available.
>
> **Anthony Robbins Companies Web site**

Skills Required: Mostly, it's all about selling. In this case, the selling of a worldview that purports to help people achieve happiness and success. It certainly has done so for millions, including those who sell it.

Duties: Pretty much the same as a life coach, but on a global scale.

Famous Examples: Handsome, charismatic Anthony Robbins, named among the Top 50 Business Intellectuals in the World by Accenture's Institute for Strategic Change, whatever that is. Robbins bases much of his work on his invention—neuroassociative conditioning, which is based on neurolinguistic programming, whatever that is.

How to Get It: Work up a drill. Make it simple. Keep it consistent. Tell people uplifting things about life, about work, about the human condition, about the prospect of success if you just work hard and think good thoughts. Try your spiel out on individuals first, then move up to dogs and cats.

The Upside: One creative burst can fuel your business for the duration. You can just do it and do it over and over again for ever bigger bucks once you get traction.

The Downside: The danger of turning into an empty hack is always there. I once attended a dinner with James Carville, who traveled all the way to the backwoods of wherever we were having our atrocious retreat. He didn't know why he was there. He was tired. The food was not so great. He had nothing to say. We were obviously bored and unhappy that he was such a dud. I didn't envy him, no matter how much money he was making that night. Oh, all right. Maybe a little.

The Dark Side: You're the only one who truly knows how full of it you really are.

Where You Go From Here: See "Infomercial Spokesperson/Celebrity Pitchman" and "Best-selling Author"; and possibly "Certified Massage Therapist."

64

Palm Reader/Psychic/Astrologer/Tarot Reader, Etc.

Predict any future you desire for the credulous

$$: $250 per hour. Unless . . . no, wait! I see the horn of Capricorn in the bumps between your lifeline and the inverted Hanged Man in the third house on the right. You're gonna do great!

ß: 178, unless you believe this nonsense, in which case, more.

Skills Required: Ability to read level of gullibility in people, and knowledge of the zodiac, palm anatomy, etc.

Duties: Ever check out one of these swamis at work? "I see a

A chart interpretation must be studied in the light of the whole, for on casual examination various traits and aspects may appear quite contradictory. The synthesis of contradictions in a chart make this study so interesting and worthy of attention to the truth seeker who ventures to take a plunge for the rest must remain content with the superficial crumbs that nature throws at them. Your

(continued)

man who is troubling you," he or she will say, "a brother perhaps." "No," the client will say, "I don't have a brother." "Well, somebody who acts as if he's a brother to you?" "I have a mechanic who takes care of my car . . ." the client will say tentatively. "That's it! A mechanic! And you have had some trouble with that car!" the seer will exclaim. And all will be revealed.

(continued from previous page)
Astro-Forecast: by careful study of a date of birth, we can know how an individual's thinking is going to be influenced at a certain date because the planets seem to affect our thoughts. Therefore it follows that thinking is destiny.

Ostaro, self-described Hindu astrologer, who has appeared on *Letterman*, on his method of reading the future in the stars

Famous Example: My favorite bullshit artist of this type is a fellow named Ostaro, who has operated on the New York City public access cable channel for decades. He wears a turban covered with stars and has a definite approach to ascertaining the future from his close reading of the zodiac. In 2002, he forecast that Martha Stewart would be convicted, as indeed she was. He has also prognosticated that Michael Jackson would be the subject of several scandals that would upset his financial apple cart, and that there would be an upsurge in interest rates in 2005, or possibly 2004, it's hard to tell. About Osama Bin Laden, he writes, "His poor circulation will lead to very complicated physical ailments." Encouraging, huh?

How to Get It: Listen to the music of the spheres.

The Upside: Always know what horse to play in the Kentucky Derby.

The Downside: People look at you funny when you go out with that weird fez on.

The Dark Side: When I was in college, I spent a few months learning how to read tarot cards, which are replete with symbols and meanings that are very ancient. I don't believe they are one bit supernatural, but in the hands of somebody on the make, much can be foretold. Anyhow, this girl in my dorm sat down for a reading. She seemed sad but otherwise okay, a condition not uncommon in college students. The first card that came up as her signifier was Death. Now, Death is a very scary card, but it means Change, not the End of Things. So I said, "You may have lost somebody very close to you recently, and it is forcing you to look at everything in a new way." She burst into tears and ran sobbing from the room. Turns out her dad had just died. And we never got to make out, either.

Where You Go from Here: The Twilight Zone.

65

Patent Troll

Purchase dead patents for peanuts, sue real company, make billions

$$: If you win, hundreds of millions per year.

ß: Off the charts. Pure bullshit in its most legalistic and malevolent form.

Skills Required: None.

Duties: The patent troll looks for patents that bear even a passing resemblance to a legitimate product. The troll then purchases that patent for, perhaps, $100,000. Armed with this patent, the troll can then go to court and get an injunction against the real company that is making the thing that slightly

> Several problems contribute to making this "patent troll" business model a simple and effective source of illegitimate profit irrespective of the quality of the patent. For example, if the troll can claim that the patent covers $5 billion in annual revenue, that troll will ask for a royalty fee of a few percentage points of revenue; e.g., $150 million per year.
>
> **David M. Simon, congressional testimony, July 24, 2003**

resembles the patent bought by the troll. The target of the troll can then make a deal for a ridiculous amount of money, paying the troll to go away, or can fight in a court system stacked to benefit the holders of patents, even illegitimate ones.

Famous Examples: NTP, which has been successful in screwing up Research In Motion, the producer of our beloved BlackBerry handheld device. Owners of a vague patent in the general neighborhood of the mighty device that has ruined and improved all of our lives, NTP, if successful, will either cost RIM billions of dollars or will simply put it out of business. Bad trolls! Bullshit trolls!

How to Get It: No talent required, other than reading the patents on file with the U.S. Patent Office. It would take a lawyer to think of this kind of scam, so make sure you either are one or are working with one. Happy hunting, disgusting, creepy troll!

The Upside: You feast on ill-gotten meat you did nothing to hunt or dress. Look at all that money you did nothing to earn!

The Downside: Almost impossible to get good PR.

The Dark Side: Hard to see. Trolls are happy to be trolls, and do not get insulted when you call them trolls or feel bad when they look in a mirror and see a plump, successful troll.

Where You Go from Here: Ogre.

66

Performance Artist

Explore the relationship between art and publicity

> The best thing about the term "performance artist" is that it includes just about everything you might want to do.
>
> **Laurie Anderson, performance artist**

$$: Nothing but notoriety, at first. But at the highest levels, where those who write about cultural events become excited about you, the detritus from the amorphous happenings you create can themselves become objects of value. And if you die? Forget about it.

ß: Hard to tell. Today's bullshit is tomorrow's culture-transforming event.

Skills Required: The ability to visualize behavior that will confound the media, garner attention, and produce artifacts that can be sold for far beyond their intrinsic value.

Duties: Say you decide that you're going to sit on a street corner and eat flies for a week as a demonstration of some concept or other. If you can articulate why in the world you want to do such a thing, you may attract the interest of media reporters who focus on the weird and unusual.

Famous Examples: Karen Finley, who performed topless while playing the cello, smeared her naked body with chocolate, and shoved yams up her rectum.

How to Get It: Just do it. A knowledge of the technology of publicity is desirable.

The Upside: In a weird way, what you do is a lot more important to defining the outer limits of culture than a host of more "serious" artists.

The Downside: Your parents don't understand what you do and feel slightly embarrassed when you're around, particularly at Thanksgiving time.

The Dark Side: Hemorrhoids.

Where You Go from Here: Reality show developer.

67

Perfume Schpritzer

Spray airborne scents at shocked passers-by

$$: Scale.

> Would you like to try some Poison today?
>
> **Perfume atomizer, Saks Fifth Avenue**

ß: 30–180; the moment when you actually hit the targets with atomized schpritz may turn into a nonbullshit confrontation.

Skills Required: Excellent coordination between thumb and forefinger.

Duties: Approach prey. Ask, "Would you like to try some ______________ today?" (Fill in the blank with the *schpritzvasser* you are dispensing.) Give one short, sharp burst of smelly mist in the air directly in front of their face. Depending on the reaction, either discuss merits of perfume in question or, for self-defense purposes, move quickly away. Repeat until quitting time.

Famous Example: Lady Perfume Sprayer, a vending machine created in 1905 that dispensed three types of scent—rose, violet, and lilac. Perfume was dispensed from the life-size figure. It was 82 inches tall and weighed 325 pounds.

How to Get It: Go to store. Fill out application. May not be either fat or unsightly.

The Upside: The next best thing to spraying grown-ups with a water gun.

The Downside: You don't get to interface with your customers for very long, and when you do they all hate you.

The Dark Side: If you schpritz the wrong person, he may hit you with his purse.

Where You Go from Here: Paintball instructor.

68

Personal Publicist

Manage the image of those who would have none without you

> This is a real, serious, loving relationship—not spur of the moment. The wedding was treated with great sobriety and seriousness.
>
> **Elliot Mintz, referring to the marriage of his client Nicky Hilton to heir Todd Meister, a marriage that lasted for eighty-six days**

$$: $5,000 to $100,000 per month, depending on the size of the client and the number of problems and opportunities created by his or her odious personality.

ß: Varies. 180, in the case of somebody like, say, Robert Blake or Scott Peterson, or 20, if you're representing a client whose business it is to get in trouble and generate their own bullshit, like Paris Hilton.

Skills Required: Be willing to stand in front of the media and get through the moment with a straight face. This is not always as easy as it looks—developing and delivering a great public rationalization for an untenable position takes a very special skill set and not a little bit of talent. Our hats are off to these primo bullshit artists!

> It is better to have a brief engagement than a short marriage.
>
> **Elliot Mintz, referring to the breakup of Kimberly Stewart, Rod Stewart's daughter, with Talan Torriero, a reality television star, whose engagement lasted for eleven days**

Duties: Protect celebrities from themselves and others. Say no to publicity opportunities that you didn't organize yourself; create an illusion of friendship and loyalty with people who are not very good at either.

Famous Example: Elliot Mintz, whose clients include and have included: John Lennon and Yoko Ono, Nicky and Paris Hilton, Bob Dylan, and Don Johnson. Mintz is peerless at managing difficult situations with terse comments that give the appearance of being bullshit-free. He has maintained protective relationships with a variety of extremely high-profile artists and celebrities, from the sublime to the ridiculous, and has weathered very public feuds with a number of agency public relations people, journalists, and other sociopaths.

How to Get It: Begin as a low-level grunt at a public relations agency dedicated to helping celebrities who need a lot of help. Make friends with your clients, handle their problems with aplomb. Pray to land a big fish that will obviate any need for further client acquisitions in the future.

The Upside: Possibility of seeing Paris Hilton naked.

The Downside: Possibility of seeing Woody Allen naked.

The Dark Side: One day your clients will be over, and then you will be, too. And nobody loves an expired publicist.

Where You Go from Here: Lecturer, Columbia School of Journalism, substituting for the tenured professor, a former blogger, when she is on vacation.

69

Personal Trainer

Build average humans into gorgeous beasts, have sex with as many as you like, marry some of them for brief periods of time

$$: $35,000 per annum. But what's the meaning of money when part of your job is holding J. Lo's foot while she tries to work out her upper thigh?

ß: 50—as high as you want.

Skills Required: Must know a series of exercises and be able to teach them to others; have loud, commanding voice to scream at people and make them push themselves to the limit; look good in weird spandex outfits so that misshapen, sad people or celebrities want to look like

> She's a gamer, that's what I would call her; she's ready for anything. You can take her through hard exercises, hard rep counts, slow cadence, whatever it is she's just right there with you. She is so considerate and she's on time and she's there to do it. She's so strong. You'd be surprised—a girl her size—how strong she is.
>
> **Gunnar Peterson, on Angelina Jolie**

you, not like themselves. Occasionally get it up on command for customers who have grown hot, sweaty, and confused during workout sessions.

> People are so busy lengthening their lives with exercise they don't have time to live them.
>
> **Jonathan Miller**

Duties: Work people out, write books that have a unique selling principle of some kind, make tapes, go on TV, sponsor machines, move to LA, meet either Jessica or Nick, decide which one you want.

Famous Examples: The field of personal training was born in the cruder, more exacting science of bodybuilding, with pioneers like Jack La Lanne, who began more than sixty years ago and is now in his early nineties and selling juicers. Before him, even, was Charles Atlas, whose advertising promised that boys who trained in his discipline would never be troubled by sand-kicking beach bullies again. More recently, there was Arnold, whose advice and example were inspirational to a generation of men, but who is now discredited because he sank to a profession even more full of bullshit than personal trainer (see Politician). Also Richard Simmons, who is now plump, which makes him look very odd in a teeny little one-piece tank top, but who has helped a legion of very fat people become slightly less fat.

How to Get It: The National Federation of Personal Trainers (NFPT), founded in 1988, offers a course in accreditation for a reasonable fee, one that is recognized by the National Commission for Certifying Agencies (NCCA), which certifies certifying agencies.

The Upside: Lookin' great, eating like a champ, swinging high and hard and loose? What a gig!

The Downside: The *San Francisco Chronicle* does a huge exposé revealing that the special additive you've been giving to your customers is, in fact, anabolic steroid. You go to jail and your clients are disgraced, in addition to having tiny, shrunken testicles.

The Dark Side: You are an overexercised monster, both bulgy and stringy at the same time, your body is aging, and so are the poor, hyperstressed clients you tend to; you wake up one morning, and God, you're tired.

Where You Go from Here: Gym teacher, middle school. Get those chubby little boys up to snuff!

70

Pet Psychic

Read minds of beloved animals,
who have no sentient thoughts,
and convey them to besotted owners,
who are in basically the same condition

> If I die before my cat, I want a little of my ashes put in his food so I can live inside him.
>
> **Drew Barrymore**

$$: $40–$100 per hour, much of which can be done on the phone. Tapes and sales of books can add significantly to the relatively minor income from this form of bullshit therapy.

ß: 199. All psychics project a load of wishes, hopes, fears, and other effluvious material onto the needy faces of those who fall within their thrall. But pet psychics come in through the soft underbelly of the soul. On the bright side, pet psychics are even more sincere than regular psychics.

Skills Required: Must love animals. Having very large hair seems to be part of the skill set also. Must also be capable of saying such things as "Dipsy is sad that he has to share your attention with Pepper" without laughing.

> Do you ever wonder what your animals are saying to you? Do you even wish you knew what they were thinking or why they have a unique behavior? Internationally acclaimed Animal Psychic Barbara Morrison has helped thousands of pet owners worldwide to gain a greater sense of understanding and appreciation for their pets by using her ability to communicate with animals. As a pet psychic and pet whisper, she lets an animal know she is listening to them, then they often have many things to say.
>
> **Barbara Morrison, pet psychic**

Duties: Consider for a moment what it means about the client that they own this particular animal. People who keep troubled gerbils may have a different profile than those who have a couple of rabid pit bulls that require understanding. Seek the need and minister to it.

Famous Example: "America's most famous and loved animal communicator," by her own admission, is Sonya Fitzpatrick. She has her own show, *The Pet Psychic,* and makes periodic appearances on talk shows and radio programs around the world.

When she was very young, her father slew her three pet geese for Christmas dinner and the little girl realized the truth—people do not have the love and understanding of animals that she had been given. Traumatized by the death of her plump, delicious (if somewhat fatty and greasy) friends, Sonya renounced her gift and determined to stop listening to the messages flowing into her from the animal kingdom. It hurt too much. But after a career in high fashion modeling in all the great capitals of Europe, Sonya moved to the United States, where, in 1994, she had what she refers to as a "spiritual experience that reopened her channels of telepathic communication with animals."

How to Get It: I have to feel that if you were gifted in this area you would probably know it already. Little sparrows would be speaking to you, and horses in the field would be gamboling over to you with information on who was going to win the third race at Hollywood Park. If instead you are not quite insane yet, do not despair. One of the great things about all psychic work, but particularly this fertile corner of the field, is that nobody can tell you you're *not* one. Just find people who are goofy about the animals they own—basically anybody with a pet—and tell them you know what little Boscobel is thinking. If they seem interested? You've got yourself a client!

The Upside: Honestly, you probably help people just as much as do chiropractors, psychiatrists, healers, and lawyers, among others. "Thank you for letting me know that

Kitty is happy and free from pain," says a testimonial from one suffering neurotic. Which helping profession can promise that kind of relief?

The Downside: When you tell people at a party that you are a pet psychic, they may have a reaction that would hurt a more sensitive animal.

The Dark Side: After years on the job, you have come to believe in your powers. And all around you, you hear beasts screaming, jibbering, complaining of their lot. See the cattle on the way to the stockyards. See that little dog dodging its way through traffic, lost. Hear the cries of the birds as they cut their way across the polluted sky! The mooing! The howling! The incessant chirping! Please, God! Make them stop!

Where You Go from Here: Bellevue.

71

Poet

Drink, write very little, diddle students, generally have license to misbehave while sponging off friends and other nonprofit organizations

> It is a sad fact about our culture that a poet can earn much more money writing or talking about his art than he can by practicing it.
>
> **W. H. Auden**

$$: $350 per annum from your actual poetry or if you're serious about a career in the business, you earn whatever college professors are making this year, plus what you get from these very cool writer-in-residence gigs you can apply for. These come with modest stipends and access to amazingly nice places to live for pretty long periods of time. Plus income from a host of grants you can get from institutions that like to sponsor poetic activities. Hey, if you're worried about wealth, you're probably not cut out to be a poet. Fame is your game.

ß: 15–155, depending on the nature of the poetry you write, and how much of it is on automatic pilot. Writing poetry that people understand and care about isn't easy, and sometimes you have to reach deep to achieve anything, always a nonbullshit proposition. On the other hand, producing little minimalist observation-ettes about Nature or aggressively minor insights about human relationships suitable for publication in *The New Yorker* or enormous opuses of dense foliage that nobody but English professors and Helen Vendler can comprehend is relatively easy. All that takes is practice.

Skills Required: Write poems, which in this culture means at least being able to lineate prose, adding odd punctuation as required. Rhyming is optional, and even, in certain free-verse cliques, frowned upon. Like this:

Write poems!
Which in this culture means at least
Being able to lineate prose adding odd
punctuation as required; rhyming

is optional and even
In certain learned circles
Frowned upon

You must also be able to generate competent and earnest prose sentences for your grant writing work, and appear appropriately "poetic" in person, a quality that is hard to teach, and has a lot to do with casual wear and placement of hair. (Whoops! Rhyming is sometimes inevitable!) You cannot appear bogus or bourgeois, which is somewhat problematic, since that's probably what you are. Aren't we all? I suggest a variety of black T-shirts and sport jackets with jeans or corduroy pants for men. The same would work for lesbian women. Gay men or straight female poets might go either for the faery gossamer thing or the elemental skirt with a leotard on top. Perhaps a shawl.

> To be a poet is a condition, not a profession.
>
> **Robert Frost**

Duties: Go hither and yon. Observe the world in all its vagaries and varieties. Speak to the deepest recesses of your soul and report back on what you find there. Sponge off friends, academic institutions, and the federal government. Find patrons and draw off their life energy until they are forced to renounce you. Bathe your liver in alcohol. Sleep with those who believe that for a moment, in sharing your ragged body, they are touching something of the firmament of the cosmos.

Famous Examples: Famous poets whose lives you may study include: Shelley, Byron, and Keats, three fabulous rock stars of the nineteenth century who sucked the grape dry and died very young; William Wordsworth, who wrote a lot of very good poetry around that same time before becoming a rich, conservative stiff, always a good career path; T. S. Eliot, who did basically the same thing; Robert Frost, the beloved uncle of American letters, who was, in reality, a really mean guy who did pretty much what he wanted to do at everybody else's expense; Billy Collins, our most famous poet right now, who writes verse that you can read and feel things about, a quality that puts him on the outs with some people, like those zany neo-formalists.

How to Get It: You must be hardworking and have a disguised ego about your stuff. This means writing poems, sending them out to places that print poetry that does not seem complete anathema to yours, taking their rejections, sending out more. If you are writing and not putting your poetry out there for people to read, you're about as much of a poet as you are a rapper because you spin rhymes in the shower. Go to poetry slams and other events where people much more terrible than you read their stuff, and read yours.

The Upside: Unlimited sex from adoring fans. The knowledge that your pain can be turned into something of artistic and/or commercial value. The right to drink all night and wake up at dusk.

The Downside: You give a reading of your work at a small lecture hall of a university that does such things. They put you up at the Travelodge. The night of the reading, you go to dinner with the head of the English department at a sad, empty place that still features a blue plate special. Eight people show up at your reading. One of them has a bottle in a brown paper bag and is dressed wrong for the season. Afterward, you go out for drinks with him.

The Dark Side: You are a dead caboose sitting empty on a neglected piece of track somewhere in a forgotten rail yard. You tell yourself that when you're dead, you will be appreciated. All things considered, that seems like a long time to wait.

Where You Go from Here: Greeting card writer.

72

Poker Teacher

Teach losers how to play cards

$$: $150,000 per year as an instructor, particularly if you get in with a bunch of celebrity patsies.

ß: 25. A very low number indeed! Why is that? Because a poker teacher is a professor of bullshit, and in terms of this book, there is quite possibly no higher profession.

> The truth of the matter is that most players are average. Some are a little better, others a little worse. But the vast majority of poker players are right there in that great, gray middle ground.
>
> **Lou Krieger, poker pro and professor**

Skills Required: If you are a male, it helps to have a truculent demeanor, be either be too thin or too fat, wear a funny hat and glasses, smoke an outlandish cigar, with a face that might just have been run over by a paving machine. Female poker instructors, on the contrary, must look hot. Leather, tight pants, a touch of bosom, all good—but what's really important is the strong whiff of sexual power that the great female sharks wield over the generally dysfunctional, somewhat asexual male nerds who occupy the table with them.

Duties: There are many poker players in the world. Most, as Lou Krieger points out, think they are good. They really aren't. What this means is that sooner or later, anybody who plays the game is periodically going to have his or her ass kicked and feel like a schmuck.

That's right. You can lose at tennis and feel: Heigh-ho! Good game! You can get squashed after four quarters on the gridiron and still come away with your manhood. But to lose at poker is to be a lame little tool. You hobble away from the table with no money and no dignity. And it all happened for reasons you just can't fathom. Why did you bet when you had no cards worth betting on? Why didn't you bet when you did? When you were trying to pass through some bullshit, why didn't anybody believe you? When you were on the level, why did everybody know it and fold? Why did the cretin across the table have your number completely triangulated all night? Why do you play this game? It's a horseshit game! The hell with it! And when can you play again, to climb back from this feeling that you're a total limp dick?

In the wake of these feelings, the nimrods who are addicted to this kind of enjoyment reach out and try to find somebody with a system, who can explain the psychology of the thing to them, a seasoned bullshit artist with an impressive set of credentials and balls to match. That could be you.

Famous Example: My favorite is Doyle Brunson because he looks like the rear end of a truck and has been at it since the Rat Pack was exploring the other side of Vegas.

How to Get It: Anybody can enter the World Series of Poker, if you've got the ante to lose. You need to be dedicated to the game, though, to get to the level where you can squeeze an honest living out of willing amateurs. You need to be able to sit at the table hour after hour, watching your money go away for a while, then come sneaking back, not lose heart, not get too high when luck is smiling, not reach for your gun to blow some wanker's head off when all you are holding is the smile between your teeth.

The Upside: No matter how you're playing, you have a steady stream of income coming in from people who think you're a winner. You may even get an occasional girl that you don't have to pay for.

The Downside: Everybody hits a bad streak now and then. When you do, your loser students all decide they want a different poker teacher.

The Dark Side: You wake up at the age of sixty alone in a fleabag somewhere off the Strip with $1.42 in your pocket and nothing but a picture of Charlie Sheen in your wallet.

Where You Go from Here: Reno. Then Branson, Missouri; then Foxwoods, Connecticut; then Atlantic City. Then the Indian reservation just off Route 20 near Willits.

73

Political Reverend

Turn public issues to personal advantage

> I think every good Christian ought to kick Falwell right in the ass.
>
> **Barry Goldwater**

$$: Millions, if you've got a good TV gig going on. A lot less, if you don't.

ß: 180.

Skills Required: Sling bullshit in the name of God. A good knowledge of Scripture is essential. The Bible seems capable of providing textual support for virtually any position, no matter how cracked.

Duties: Select issues that you can be heard on. Harangue people on the subject in order to achieve some form of profit for yourself. This can be in the form of money, naturally, but political influence is also an excellent form of remuneration, since that often can be turned into hard cash. Jesse Jackson, for example, has a synergistic relationship with his operating arm, the Rainbow/PUSH Coalition, which raises legitimate issues in the public sector, then goes behind the scenes to politely requisition contributions from wealthy corporations.

Famous Examples: Billy Graham, Pat Robertson, and Jerry Falwell have all made tremendous hay staying tight with the ruling party. Falwell in particular has had a mighty run stretching back decades, and was quoted not long ago bragging that Karl Rove always returns his telephone calls. No, duh.

How to Get It: It's a little-known fact that you can be a reverend by saying you are one. Once you've set up that collection plate, find a place that will listen to you every Sunday. I just passed through a town in California that had a population of 384 people. I counted five churches there. Once that's established, reach out to the media and find reporters who find you amusing. Now choose your positions wisely—race, sin, godless Democrats. Start local, aim global. And good luck. No, wait, you don't need luck. God may be busy making earthquakes near Al Qaeda headquarters, but he still has time to watch out for you. You're his man!

The Upside: All kinds of people hugging you, throwing money at you.

The Downside: You have to be careful when you check into that motel with Lurleen.

The Dark Side: What do you mean, the IRS is on line two?

Where You Go from Here: Dinner at the White House. They're happy with your latest broadcast and need somebody to sit next to Bill O'Reilly.

74

Politician

Represent the interests of those who will pay to get you elected

$$: 127,500 tops, if you're honest. Maybe less, if you stay local, or more, if you're bullshitting the entire nation.

> In politics, stupidity is not a handicap.
>
> **Napoleon Bonaparte**

ß: 12–190. American politics has always been replete with bullshit, but in the last fifty years, it's been out of control. In the 1950s, it was a dark black pile and rose so high that it actually smothered quite a few people. In the 1960s, there was a ton of it around, but also huge pockets of fresh air if you cared to look for it, and by the time it was morning in America, bullshit had hit levels unprecedented since the late nineteenth century, when Reconstruction devolved into a politician's right to print money.

Skills Required: Walk and chew gum at the same time.

Duties: Saying one thing and meaning another; promising one thing and then doing another; talking out of both sides of your mouth; prosecuting immoral slugs from the other party while your guys are buggering pages in the cloakroom; pursuing narrow agendas that will make your friends a lot of money; drinking at the right clubs.

> No diet will remove all the fat from your body, because the brain is entirely fat. Without a brain, you might look good, but all you could do is run for public office.
>
> **George Bernard Shaw**

Famous Examples: Rome did it better than just about anybody else. Cicero. Caesar. Augustus. Marcus Aurelius, a first-class general, philosopher, and leader. The art of politics in Rome was the practice that elevated the great leaders from the crazy bastards who killed their own mothers and baked their enemies into pies. It was politics that represented the best of that civilization.

Later, you had towering geniuses in the field like Washington, Jefferson, Hamilton, Monroe, Madison—the mostly young men who tied philosophy to revolution and built our nation without turning into a bunch of murderous maniacs like the nutty French; in Britain, there were Gladstone and Disraeli and Churchill, who stood up to Hitler and the Fascists within his own empire while downing a complete bottle of brandy before noon every day. I also happen to like Eisenhower, who kept the Allies united during the Second World War and went on to run one of the most peaceful and prosperous decades in American history and got us out of Korea for the most part.

At this point we get too close to our own time for me to annoy you by talking too much about it. I don't think we're writing any big chapters in world history on the political front, let me put it that way.

How to Get It: From the beginning, you should probably choose which portion of the populace you want to represent. In my town, for example, there are politicians who simply decided a long time ago that they speak for those who want to pay the lowest taxes possible and don't care about the impact that will have on schools, libraries, public transportation. Others made a choice to align themselves with union members or black people or Orthodox Jews or wealthy golfers who want to expand their links. In microcosm, this is the bullshit game that all politicians play, and to some extent it makes sense. Like our legal system, it pits all points of view, ostensibly, in a fair fight. Except, you know, only some constituencies have money. I mean, there's that.

The Upside: You are a respected member of your community, your nation, and the world. People voted for you. What a rush!

The Downside: Hour after hour after hour after hour of debate on other people's crap. Who gives a shit about highway funding in West Virginia! Christ!

The Dark Side: You said there were weapons of mass destruction, and you knew there were not. That's kind of fucked up.

Where You Go from Here: Either dogcatcher or the Council on Foreign Relations.

75

Pollster/Market Researcher

Ask a stupid question, you get a stupid answer

$$: $28,000 for entry-level query jockeys. At the upper levels are those who analyze data to give those who pay for it the general message they want to hear.

> A public-opinion poll is no substitute for thought.
>
> **Warren Buffett**
>
> Is it ignorance or apathy? Hey, I don't know and I don't care.
>
> **Jimmy Buffett**

ß: 63 percent of respondents are really sick of market research that claims to know what they are thinking. The other 33 percent don't have an opinion.

Skills Required: Must be very skillful at constructing research tools that formulate questions in the exact way that will return desired responses. Must be adept at principles of statistics and low-level mathematics, so that information can be manipulated by marketers and political operatives into whatever shape they desire. A degree in psychology is not mandatory but helpful.

Duties: This is one of the more interesting occupations for those who take their bullshit seriously and like to see how it plays out in the real world. Process, attention to detail, and a solemn demeanor are essential as the pollster moves forward to draw in clients, ascertain their needs, design the tools to elicit data from the bored and witless populace, and then report them in usable form. In the case of political pollsters, the duties are even more fascinating, as pollsters work to find pockets of opinion that can be exploited by the spin doctors who run politicians in search of opinions they can strongly hold.

Famous Examples: Elmo Roper, who was born with the twentieth century in the year of 1900, is believed to have invented the modern practice of polling. Lou Harris was the first pollster, working for John F. Kennedy, who designed an entire campaign around state-by-state research. Today, polling continues throughout the land, pumping a horde of bullshit opinions into the marketplace that are essential to a plethora of bullshit endeavors and very few nonbullshit ones.

How to Get It: Get a BS, which is appropriate. After that, you'll need a tweedy or otherwise conservative look. Try bow ties—I know they look kind of gay, but they may help you gain that intellectual gravitas you know you sorely lack. The demand for what you do is acute and will not go away as long as the forces of medieval Islam do not succeed in supplanting our form of worship with theirs.

The Upside: Your work moves the culture. Sure, it's tedious and grueling and tedious, with tons of tedious paper and tedious spreadsheets and tedious data by the bucketful flowing down your leg all the time. But you like that!

The Downside: Sometimes other people seem bored when you talk with them about your interesting work.

The Dark Side: You become increasingly relativistic and incapable of coming to any conclusions that you didn't already hold in advance. You also smell of pipe tobacco, moldy slipper material, and aftershave, which you acquired based on confidential market research that showed it had a positive effect on your credibility with people who earn more than $150,000 per year.

Where You Go from Here: An underground lab at Pepperdine, where the next president is right now being grown from a small pod submerged in amniotic fluid.

76

Pop Tart

Produce product for music industry; become product for publicity industry

> I get to go to lots of overseas places, like Canada.
>
> **Britney Spears**

$$: You enter at the top of the pile. Just make sure you have a good business manager, possibly one who is not your mother.

ß: 10–99. In the beginning, they work you hard. Later, you can't let out a squeak without somebody being up your butt. But the money is exceptional, the work pretty easy once you learn the steps.

Skills Required: Must be young, supple, and have a beautiful body that can be the repository of the fantasies of millions of men and women.

Duties: Make CDs and music videos, appear in awards ceremonies, marry inappropriate individuals for brief periods of time, have public embarrassments as necessary.

Famous Example: Britney, who embodies all the virtues of the successful pop tart in one package, from her borderline scandalous beginnings to her nutty five-minute marriage to some other Jason Alexander, to her current run as mommy dearest to Scruffy-boy (see Backup Dancer).

> Butterflies are always following me, everywhere I go.
>
> **Mariah Carey**

How to Get It: Many of the current crop of pop tarts started out working as cast members for Disney in their Mouseketeer division. It's possible, however, that you may need a borderline psychotic mother and/or father to stoke the furnace here.

The Upside: You are angry! You are vain! You are everybody's idol! You stalk off stages when you are annoyed! You take hundreds of lovers! You are fabulous! You are you!

The Downside: You have no childhood. You are taught to have no shame. The people you love abuse and use you. Your fans let you down the moment you show an ounce of body fat.

The Dark Side: You can't fit into that size 22 gown they bought for you at the last Grammys.

Where You Go from Here: Seclusion.

77

Posse Dude

Stand around looking large

$$: Small cheddar, until you get your own jam.

ß: 180, unless they shoot you, then it quickly goes down to the low single digits. Prison is also a minimum bullshit facility.

Skills Required: Ability to stand around looking menacing is a must. Not long ago, I was over at a television setup, honking on some bullshit for the corporation, and who should be doing a satellite interview tour in the next studio but 50 Cent, whose name, for those who are not fuckin' ignorant assholes (see right) is pro-

> The Group of the biggest, fakest, bitches on earth. 50cent and The Game had a fake beef to get publicity for their new albums coming. What kind of fuckin ignorant asshole says how he kills and fucks people up when he dosent know shit about it? All he does is sit at his mansion all day gettin drunk watch shows on his big screen TV, then tries to come off like he's from the ghetto and caps motherfuckers up everynight, when this faget wouldnt even touch a paintball gun.
>
> **211JBHoodz defines the G-Unit for the Urban Dictionary**

nounced Fitty, or Fif, for short. Anyhow, Fif is in the studio, laying down what looks to be some ill-tempered personal publicity jive, and a whole bunch of his posse dudes are in the greenroom waiting for the Man, eating fruit and muffins and doing their best to look as bad as they can in a spot owned and operated by Reuters. Outside the studio door between me and the bathroom is this guy, must be maybe six foot eight, 420 pounds. And I try to get by him because, you know, the bathroom is right there, and he says, "Hey." That's all he says. So I went downstairs to the bathroom on another floor.

Duties: Whatever 50, Dogg, or most importantly, Dre may have in mind for you. Park cars. Go to the bank for Mr. Banks, or get some yayo or herb for Yayo and Herb. Take a bullet or deliver one as necessary. And the whole time work on your own groove, so you can have your own Unit one of these days. The true, respected hip-hop artist must maintain a double life, with strong street bona fides and the ability, like Rimbaud and Caravaggio, to turn a gangster's life into art. No street cred, you're suspect, and there's nothing that can give you that faster than a stint with the posse, particularly one that lands you in the can.

Famous Examples: 50 Cent's G-Unit, short for Guerrilla Unit, made up of 50 himself, who's tight with Dre, as anybody in this part of the world has to be, plus Tony Yayo, Lloyd Banks, Young Buck, and Game, who joined and then had a very public feud with 50 in order to promote his Dre-produced CD. The posse also has an official DJ, DJ Whoo Kid. G-Unit raps about drugs, sex, and helping endangered species of monkeys in the rain forest.

How to Get It: Yayo met Fif when they were both kids on the South Side of Queens. "50, he could see in me that I live, and we both rapped too, so it was just a natural friendship," he says. "So we started working together on the street and then when he started taking rap more seriously he took me along too 'cause he knew I was nice." Being nice, then, is important.

Yayo spent the '90s on the battle circuit, honing his craft by heaping invective on the competition (see *8 Mile* for a good example of this perilous art form), and when 50 took his famous nine slugs, which did not kill him but were definitely *not* bullshit, Yayo hung in there with him, and afterward, when everything started to fall into place for Fif and the G-Unit was formed and the whole thing was cooking, Yayo got hit with a gun charge, which was inconvenient, seeing how well everything was going. Dodging the law for as long as he could, he recorded a bunch of tracks, got closer to Eminem and Dre, started laying down plans for the CD that would become *Thoughts of a Predicate Felon*. In December 2002, he was finally apprehended by the NYPD at the Copa and went inside. While he was doing his time, the G-Unit delayed the release of a number of projects so that Yayo could get a verse onto them, proving that the posse is not just a family, not just a business entity supporting one main guy, but is, instead, a little repertory company of artists that hang together, appear in one another's work, support one another, and work for one another's success. In a bullshit world, that counts for something.

The Upside: Blunts, bitches, and ho's? I'm just guessing.

The Downside: Hurts really bad when you get shot . . .

The Dark Side: . . . and die.

Where You Go from Here: The Vibe Awards. Then, immediately after your appearance informs the police of your whereabouts, Folsom.

78

Postmodern Artist

Provide corporate and industrial art for those in need of interior decoration

$$: $0–$250,000 per picture and up, more when you're dead.

ß: 94.

Skills Required: Open can; wield brush, fingers, and other appendages to produce objects that fill space. Must be able to read up on current trends in corporate interior design and deliver on specific vision of senior executives and the art brokers who serve their needs.

Duties: Provide canvases and sculptures that give the appearance of being art without the

> **FREDERICK**
> I'm not interested in what your interior decorator would think, okay?!
>
> **DUSTY**
> Well, I can't commit to anything without consulting her first. That's what I have her for, okay?
>
> **FREDERICK**
> This is degrading! You don't buy paintings to blend in with the sofa!
>
> **DUSTY**
> It's not a sofa, it's an ottoman!
>
> **Woody Allen,**
> ***Hannah and Her Sisters***

attendant discomfort that often ruins the enjoyment of artistic creations by bourgeoisie who pay good money to make sure the areas in which they live and work are tasteful and beautiful.

> But the term "reality," always ambiguous when used in connection with art, has never been used more ambiguously than here. A piece of imitation-woodgrain wallpaper is not more "real" under any definition, or closer to nature, than a painted simulation of it; nor is wallpaper, oilcloth, newspaper or wood more "real," or closer to nature, than paint on canvas.
>
> **Clement Greenberg**

Famous Examples: Jeff Koons, who made paintings and sculptures of himself having sex with his Italian porn-star wife, La Cicciolina, which was interesting, not edifying; Mark Kostabi, whose name should be here; and my favorite, Ad Reinhardt, who is in every museum with large paintings that, if you stare at them for a long time, will reveal different shades of black, some of which are very black, indeed.

How to Get It: The Internet is filled with crass, commercial Web sites that offer a host of space-filling exercises by nameless copycats; there is clearly a market for this stuff so you could easily become one of those. This, however, is nowhere near as satisfying as being a "real" artist, whose name alone gleans hundreds of thousands of dollars for objects that would be worthless without that signature attached.

A huge breakthrough was made in the early part of the last century, when master bullshitter Marcel Duchamp signed a urinal, which was immediately recognized as an act of genius. After Duchamp, the next tremendous step forward in the creation of the form came with the work of Jackson Pollock, whose canvases—large, full of energy, paint, and pee—had absolutely no meaning to anyone who had not read the criticism associated with them.

Later artists like Clyfford Still and Mark Rothko pushed the envelope even further, exploring the realms where artwork was little more than vacant musings on color and the quality of canvas, and the skills involved were so minimal that anyone wishing to wade into the lucrative pool could do so with impunity. The great benefit of abstract expressionist artwork is that it conveys the impression of sophistication, but has no content at all other than what the broker/critic asserts for it. This makes it perfect for a corporate setting. It is also often quite large, rendering it excellent for boardrooms, hallways, and executive offices.

The Upside: Wealth, honor, and groupies that range from nubile young acolytes to hirsute, porcine critics.

The Downside: Ugly stalkers.

The Dark Side: The knowledge that you are a hack, which can only be eradicated through constant applications of alcohol.

Where You Go from Here: Curatorship at the Tate in London.

79

Quantum Physicist/ String Theorist

Produce theories about the nature of the universe that are not amenable to proof by normal human means

> The more success the quantum theory has, the sillier it looks.
>
> **Albert Einstein**

$$: Academic professor salary. If you become a cultural icon, like Brian Greene or Stephen Hawking, you can be one of the few who attain rock star status equal to that of, say, the host of a popular cooking show.

ß: 0–60 in 4.8 seconds, like a Corvette, but in negative time/space.

Skills Required: Bullshit at such a high level of discourse, with such a profound understanding of arcane mathematical concepts, that everybody thinks they are stupider than you.

Duties: Describe this universe and either two others, three others, nine others, or eleven others, if you count the Mall of America.

Famous Examples: So many! It's an industry. Niels Bohr, who explored the fact that light can be both a particle and a wave at the same time; Werner Heisenberg, who found that everything is made uncertain simply by the fact that we study it; more recently, the string theorists, who have now broken up into two warring camps, each fighting for control of PBS. One school says there are many, many universes, possibly an infinite number. The other school is more conservative and counts just a couple of cosmic alternatives, and has the benefit of being represented by a total babe.

> We have reversed the usual classical notion that the independent "elementary parts" of the world are the fundamental reality, and that the various systems are merely particular contingent forms and arrangements of these parts. Rather, we say that inseparable quantum interconnectedness of the whole universe is the fundamental reality, and that relatively independently behaving parts are merely particular and contingent forms within this whole.
>
> **David Bohm and B. J. Hiley, "On the Intuitive Understanding of Nonlocality as Implied by Quantum Theory," 1975**

How to Get It: Like plastic surgeons, divorce lawyers, and other high-level performers, bullshit artists in the science game need to jump through a few hoops before they earn the right to practice their craft with impunity. You have to be good at math, for one thing, and we're not talking about arithmetic, either, or even trig. We're in the field where guys draw weird arrows all over the place. That's a big hump for a lot of us. But if math doesn't scare you, proceed to acquire other nonessential knowledge through college, graduate work, and postgraduate work. After that comes post-postgraduate work, which then delivers you into the rare portion of the population which, at the age of thirty, has never existed outside of school from the time they were three.

The Upside: In your hands you hold the secret to the machinery that runs the universe. That's heady stuff, which is good—because you're a head case, dude! But seriously. The media loves you. Your last book was a best seller that everyone bought but nobody read, which, as you know, is the very best kind. And while other guys from your class are playing with petri dishes, you're accelerating fictional particles at hyperspeed underneath the mountains of Switzerland.

The Downside: None of what you do helps anybody understand anything.

The Dark Side: Tomorrow . . . next week . . . perhaps a year or two from now . . . some sharp kid is going to come along with a theory that takes a wicked detour directly from Einstein, goes completely around quantum theory, and explains the entire universe in simple, elegant terms that do not need a billion-dollar machine to prove. Your entire realm of endeavor will be relegated to a footnote on the twentieth century, the way the nineteenth was obsessed with phrenology—the science of reading head bumps.

Where You Go from Here: Writer of questions for *Jeopardy!*

80

Raw Chef

Give other people food designed solely for the purpose of keeping them regular

> Eat it raw.
>
> **Anonymous**

$$: $12,400, unless you own your own restaurant. Even then, the money is not great. Your materials are expensive. Your clientele is not always the most affluent, and they take a long time to chew their food—that ties up tables.

ß: 98. The occasional dish you present to people can be eaten and enjoyed. But cheer up. Nobody is perfect.

Skills Required: Zen slicing. Tantric dicing. The ability to arrange inedible objects in such a way as to make them appear delicious.

Duties: The raw chef is mostly to be found in portions of our nation where the loose marbles have rolled and common sense has yet to find them—California. The Hudson Valley of New York State. The portions of the Pacific

Northwest where coffee and bizarre teas have become a religion. Sedona, Taos, and other rich hipster towns in the Southwest. Gay or collegiate pockets of less enlightened urban areas. Those who eat raw, not accidentally but as a way of life, are unified by one common attribute: they view food as a form of laxative. Perhaps that sounds a bit stark. Let me put it another way. Raw eaters view the food they eat as a necessary tool in their ongoing fight to have regular, satisfactory bowel movements. So if you are a raw chef, it is your duty to make that possible for them in the most humane, attractive, and, yes, rigorous way possible.

Famous Examples: Will Keith and John Harvey Kellogg, from Battle Creek, Michigan, believed that "the best to you each morning" meant eating mounds of fiber in the form of breakfast cereals, with predictable results.

How to Get It: There are cooking schools for raw chefs throughout the United States. My favorite boasts an instructor named VeRAWnika. I ate at a friend's house a few months ago, a guy who has his own raw chef assigned to prepare all his meals. The dinner was interesting. We began with a root vegetable soup of some kind that was quite tasty, although it did have that characteristic uncooked edge to it; it was quite well seasoned and had a nice consistency that is impossible to describe. Creamy but gritty. The main course featured a variety of vegetable piles, including something that looked like spaghetti but wasn't, and was bland but also very moist. The one thing I really liked on the plate was a risotto redolent of tamarind, cumin, and coriander, which turned out to have been, in fact, cooked, in deference to our status as untutored guests of the establishment: Dessert looked like a chocolate sundae, but was instead a very nice arrangement of raw cocoa flavored with honey, dates, and spices unknown. After dinner, we had a nice conversation with our hosts until my companion complained of a stomachache that eventually lasted for a couple of days. Maybe practiced rawsters don't have that reaction, but I'm not sure. Maybe they're looking for it.

The Upside: Did you love to make mud pies as a child? Objects that appeared delectable but were in fact inorganic and undigestible? If so, rejoice. How much would any of us give to make our living from the things we loved to do when we were little?

The Downside: Tastes change. In a couple of years you may be called upon to celebrate this living planet of ours just a little bit less and start cooking innocent, dead animals in order to make a living.

The Dark Side: One of your very special clients becomes crazed with a desire for nonraw, nonvegan, nonorganic, nonlocal food, and goes to McDonald's for a double quarter pounder with cheese, eats it, goes into shock from all those toxins, and dies.

Where You Go from Here: Your body decorporealizes, and you disappear one morning in a flash of gas.

81

Realtor

Do nothing till you hear from me

> One man's ceiling is another man's floor.
>
> **Paul Simon**

$$: $27,500–$350,000. What's the price of a starter castle in your area?

ß: 47–156.

Skills Required: Completely bullshit people about the value of the home they are thinking of buying.

Duties: Make each shack a bungalow, every small tract house a charming fixer-upper, every dilapidated pile of steaming junk a diamond in the rough.

Famous Example: I like the guys who sold developers the property for the gigantic Palisades Mall in Rockland County, New York, right over the Tappan Zee Bridge. The entire structure is now sinking into the soggy heart of the planet. Good work, gentlemen! I won't mention your names because I think you might also be in the waste management business!

How to Get It: It's pretty easy to become a local realtor. If you clean up well, can talk a blue streak, be extremely pleasant and easy while selling, you can drop by your local real estate broker and apply for a job. They may want you to have a license of some sort. If so, get one. It's no big deal, obviously. Have you met a realtor?

The Upside: Easy work, very close to home. Nobody ever really knows where you are.

The Downside: You work with the Krupniks to find them their perfect dream home—dozens of hours over four months!—and then they go with Fran Winkler and buy that dump on Crane Street that was privately listed! Is there no fairness? No loyalty?

The Dark Side: You sell the cat lady's house to the Vierras, and two weeks later the cat pee smell is back and now Mr. Vierra seems not to be such a nice guy after all. And he knows where you live.

Where You Go from Here: Under the end zone at Giants Stadium.

82

Right-Wing Radio Talk Show Host

Entertain millions of listeners while helping them feel good about their prejudices

> Right you are if you think you are.
>
> **Pirandello**

$$: Zillions.

ß: 199.9

Skills Required: Must be able to hate a wide variety of people, places, and things, and pass along that enormous capacity to others, stoking the overall level of hatred in our society to ever-greater heights.

Duties: Spew invective and animus every day, for four to six hours per day, obsessing and perseverating on the objects and subjects you despise over and over and over again.

Famous Examples: Come on. You know who I'm talking about. But he's not the only one. Turn on your radio and make your way around the dial. My pal Lenny came back from Thanksgiving with his parents last year, sad and appalled. "They used to be reasonable people," he says. "Now I don't know. Since they started listening to the talk shows on radio, they're intolerant, won't agree to disagree about anything, get mad right away, start screaming at people and calling them names." It isn't only children who are influenced by what they see and hear in the media.

How to Get It: There are all kinds of ways. In the old days, you had to come up through local radio, either as a sane broadcaster who could then turn into a splenetic, egotistical weapon of hatred, or as a small-market nut who caught on. Now that the Internet has become a legitimate way to get your message out into the willing, servile mass media, it is possible to blog and podcast your way into the tiny, enraged hearts of millions.

The Upside: It feels good to spew.

The Downside: You have an ulcer the size of a quarter eating a hole in your gut.

The Dark Side: Somebody finds out about the pink taffeta tutu you wear while you're broadcasting every day.

Where You Go from Here: Satellite radio for hundreds of millions of dollars, if it's still around.

83

Ringmaster

Wear top hat, strut around

$$: $250 per week, unless you're with the big show. Then more, but not as much as you might think. Nobody remembers the ringmaster. The lion tamer, sure! The elephant handler! Even the clowns! But the ringmaster, who holds the whole thing together, is completely and totally fungible.

> Wanted: Ringmaster for Boccaccio Brothers' Circus; eight shows per week, must be able to sing over loud background noise and devote at least 60 hours per week to various offstage duties throughout February and March. Respond Box 222, Boston Station, MA.
>
> **Classified ad, *Show Business* magazine, circa 1980**

ß: 111, due to the repetitive nature of the gig, the number of shows you do per day, the circumstances under which you perform, and the assholes you have to keep in line, including your own management. It's like being a corporate controller, except the fat cats you deal with smell worse, for the most part.

Skills Required: Must look good in outrageous swallow-tail coats of various materials, be able to sing a few songs, look respectable in large headwear, bellow instructions upon request.

Duties: Hold circus show together by directing the attention of Ladeeeeeees and Gentlemen! to whatever ring the action is going on in; present vapid tunes that accompany entry and exit of animals and trainers; shout over exploding stuff. Also helps to set up and break down enormous sets and gear for the show, which is, actually, 75 percent of the circus performer's life.

Famous Examples: None. That's the thing.

How to Get It: A long time ago, I answered an ad in a magazine I used to read in order to get jobs, the kind with ink that comes off on your hands. A couple of days later, I received a phone call telling me to go down to a place called the Boston Arena, which is not there anymore. This was to be the winter home of an operation I'll call the Boccaccio Brothers' Circus, although that was not its name, although it's not far off and was, in truth, managed by two hapless Italian brothers who had circus in their blood. I got the job of ringmaster.

I sang "Be a Clown," the national anthem, and a few more related tunes throughout the show, and said,

"Ladeeeeeees and Gentlemen!" more times than I care to count, and made friends with a bunch of clowns, including a really cute girl who, unsurprisingly, had a terrific sense of humor, and a German elephant handler, who was one of the coolest people I have ever known. The lion tamer was a jerk, but that's kind of what you'd expect, huh? I loved the smell of sawdust and the feeling of arriving at a great space that would soon fill up with people. Sadly, it didn't fill up with enough people, and on the last day of our run the Boccaccio Brothers showed all the signs of wanting to abscond with the box office take without parting with any for us, the performers.

So it came to pass that I was spokesman at one of the weirdest business meetings I have ever attended. Paul Boccaccio was sitting behind his desk, very sweaty, interrupted during packing up. We all filed in—the techs who set up the gear, the clowns—a sorry, sad-sack bunch, I must say—and about 5,000 pounds of elephant, lion, tiger, and bear handlers, most from Eastern Europe, and me. "Paul," I said, because I had the best English, "we're not letting you out of the office until we've all been paid." There followed a vast amount of squealing, and cajoling. It seemed that if we were paid, the Boccaccio Brothers would see no profit from the entire run of the show and might even take a loss. There was more of that. I finally said, "I can control the clowns, Paul, but I can't say the same for the elephant and bear guys." These latter had been instructed to say nothing, but look very angry and fierce, which was not far from the truth. "They're going to punch you until we get our money," I added. And so we were paid. And I learned an important lesson about bullshit artists. If you punch them, they will give.

The Upside: The lights! The roar of the crowd! The fun of being with people who are completely dedicated about what they do.

The Downside: The eighth show of the week can be a real drain. And also, you know, it ends, and you are just a guy who did that once and must get a real bullshit job where you don't get to wear a cool hat.

The Dark Side: The circus life is not for everybody. And it incapacitates you for real life. Old ringmasters become stagehands. Or, if they have some talents beyond those necessary for being a ringmaster, clowns.

Where You Go from Here: Guy who calls people with the electronic leg irons to their table at the Outback Steakhouse.

84

Roadkill Collector

Cruise highways looking for dead things

> Either you laugh it off, or you puke.
>
> **Anonymous roadkill collector, MTV**

$$: Minimum wage. What do you expect for a job where you get to work outside all day, nobody bothers you, and job security is excellent?

ß: 120, and once you get used to it, much lower.

Skills Required: Travel your territory. Spot dramatically dead stuff strewn all over the highway, scoop it up, go out for drinks aplenty after work!

Duties: I just tole you!

Famous Examples: Well, not that many, per se, but that don't make it not worth doing. Not everybody wants the limelight, you know.

How to Get It: It's rough. They got this examination you gotta take in order to be a board-certified roadkill collector. And the field test is no walk on the parkway, believe you me!

The Upside: You are doing your part to make America beautiful.

The Downside: Ironically, the small animals that break apart on contact are the worst.

The Dark Side: Sometimes you don't want to get up in the morning.

Where You Go from Here: Ombudsman, *The New York Times.*

85

Rock Star

Live fast, die old,
leave a really desiccated corpse

> They die in youth, and their life is among the unclean.
>
> **Job 36; 5–6, 14**

$$: The hits just keep on comin'!

ß: Dude!

Skills Required: If you're young, trash shit. If you're old, stay skinny and leathery.

Duties: Get out on the road, do the funky chicken, trade in wife for new model every couple of years.

Famous Examples: Mick and Rod and Steve and Pete and Roger and Bobby—Bobby, man, who got so weird!

How to Get It: There's a big difference between being a musician and being a rock star. I mean, like, there are a lot of musicians around, and that's fine, but there aren't that many true rock stars, who are alive, at any rate, and you don't want to be a dead one! That's no fun! In fact, here, from our friends at Dial-the-Truth Ministries, is a sobering list of what happened to 221 rock stars who have bought the ranch over the years:

The Leading Causes of Death Among Rock Stars

Assorted crashes	77	Electrocution	3
Murdered/Suicide	54	Choking	2
Drug and alcohol related	49		
Various diseases	36	Total deaths	221

The Upside: Drinking! Singing! Screwing!

The Downside: You can't remember any of it.

The Dark Side: One day the phone rings . . . and it's Time Life Music . . . and they're doing a "where are they now" boxed set . . . and they want to know if you'd like to host the infomercial . . . and you say yes. As long as you can wear a cap.

> Of all the things I've ever lost I miss my mind the most.
>
> **Steven Tyler, Aerosmith**

Where You Go from Here: Judge, *American Idol* rip-off on Bravo.

86

Rogue Journalist

Work the system untroubled by annoying self-doubts entertained by others, misuse the confidence placed in you by your subjects, nurture book deals

$$: $75,000–$100,000.

ß: 150.

Skills Required: Must be able to write faction.

> I have to remind my dad, "Journalists—no matter how many cigars they smoke with you—are not your friends, so don't talk to them."
>
> **Cameron Diaz**

Duties: The life of a regular old reporter is depressingly devoid of bullshit, unless you count the binge drinking. Bullshit reporters, on the other hand, have it a lot easier. They begin with a story line from the outset—one usually arrived at with their editors. They cozy up to a small circle of well-polished quote monkeys who give them what they want to hear: security analysts, college professors, interested competitors, political opponents. There are a million ways an editor and journalist can team up to write a compelling, entertaining, superficially balanced piece that makes a nod at journalism as it whizzes by toward another destination entirely.

> The man who reads nothing at all is better educated than the man who reads nothing but newspapers.
>
> **Thomas Jefferson**

Famous Examples: Judith Miller of *The New York Times,* who spoke with just the right people in order to report on the many weapons of mass destruction lurking in Saddam's closet; Jayson Blair, who bagged the whole source thing entirely and just made a bunch of stuff up. *The Washington Post. The New Republic. USA Today.* Every news organization of value has had one or two. As long as reporters are allowed to write pieces that rely solely on bullshit unnamed sources, it will be difficult for them to see why they shouldn't also utilize totally fictional ones.

How to Get It: One must establish solid superstar status to get the Woodward-Bernstein Chair in any news organization. Stephen Glass of *The New Republic* was one such. Having

> I believe in equality for everyone, except reporters and photographers.
>
> **Gandhi**

shone bright in his early days, he used to sit at staff meetings, hypnotizing his colleagues and editors with tales of great stories he was working on; in the end it was the need to protect those lies that made him tell even bigger ones.

> Seven weeks into an examination of former *USA Today* reporter Jack Kelley's work, a team of journalists has found strong evidence that Kelley fabricated substantial portions of at least eight major stories, lifted nearly two dozen quotes or other material from competing publications, lied in speeches he gave for the newspaper and conspired to mislead those investigating his work.
>
> ***USA Today*, March 19, 2004**

The Upside: The mighty of the earth tremble when you walk into the room.

The Downside: Jeez, it's hard to slip a bogus factoid into a piece now. People are watching!

The Dark Side: Disgraced. You are as much of a nonperson as any character you ever created.

Where You Go from Here: You can be a very good blogger.

Royalty/Heir

Bow and wave, endure scandals

> I sometimes wonder if two-thirds of the globe is covered in red carpet.
>
> **Prince Charles**

$$: You don't need money because your face is on it.

ß: 105.

Skills Required: Presiding, attending, not being caught picking your nose; must know how to bow, curtsy properly, and dance with people grotesquely taller, shorter, fatter, or smellier than you are, which is likely because everyone is pretty much smellier than you are.

Duties: Cut ribbons, attend presentations, eat lots of dinners while still being able to fit into a 300-year-old suit, drink tons of booze without getting visibly drunk, must produce heir that marries another heir or Paris Hilton.

Famous Examples: The Windsors, the Grimaldis, the Jaggers.

How to Get It: Be born into it or marry into it, either by being a celebrity (Grace Kelly) or by stealing your sister's boyfriend (Diana Spencer).

> Being a princess is not all it's cracked up to be.
>
> **Princess Diana**

The Upside: Get to wear lots of velvet, if that's your thing.

The Downside: People think you're shallow and inbred.

The Dark Side: You *are* shallow and inbred.

Where You Go from Here: Diet commercials.

Spin Doctor

Position stuff

> On the other hand . . .
>
> Tevye

$$: $65,000–$1.25 million.

ß: 27–163. When things are good, they are very very good. And when they're bad, they call you.

Skills Required: Must be able to articulate complicated thoughts, ideas, and positions with such elegance that people forget what they were angry about.

Duties: Make chicken salad out of chickenshit.

Famous Example: Howard Rubenstein. Howard has seen it all, so nothing fazes him. That's an invaluable quality when everybody around you is screaming because their hair is on fire.

How to Get It: Part witch doctor, media analyst, and psychoanalyst, this arcane professional lives, like a panda, off the tough vegetable material other animals would choke on: Divorce. Murder. Grotesque sexual revelations. Illegal use of power. An onslaught of gossips seeking fresh, bloody meat to devour . . .

> Ninety percent of the game is half mental.
>
> **Yogi Berra**

If you wish to become a doctor of spin, you must begin your career as a crisis manager very early. When you are young, you must be seen as a person who can come up with solutions when everybody else is running for the exits. And you must be brilliant and ruthless. The line between strategist, spin doctor, and hit man is often vague, as even the very best friends of Karl Rove will tell you.

The Upside: Spin doctors are like pythons. They eat very well at each meal, and then rest for long periods afterward.

The Downside: Must listen to amazing waves of obnoxious whining from rich clients.

The Dark Side: Phil Spector is waiting in your reception area.

Where You Go from Here: A six-month silent retreat at a Zen monastery.

89

Sports Bloviator

Delve deep into a bottomless river of drivel

> I'm tired of hearing about money, money, money, money. I just want to play the game, drink Pepsi, wear Reebok.
>
> **Shaquille O'Neal**

$$: Radio guys make less than those on TV, but a fair number do both and pile up a huge wad.

ß: 140. And you can talk about that number all day!

Skills Required: Brain must be cleared of all extraneous material to make room for withering blizzard of sports dates, names, places, salaries, and other effluvia.

Duties: Radio bloviators must talk with crazy callers and hold strong opinions on every franchise in town; on television, the same is true, but your bloviating time is shorter. The real trick is when you're off duty. If you can stop talking about sports—professional, amateur, high school, middle school, grade school—you're not a real sports bloviator.

Famous Example: A few years ago, I flew to Europe seated next to one of the great sports announcers and commentators of our time. He's a very nice person. The flight was more than nine hours long. After about four hours, I was ready to stab myself with a plastic fork. Baseball. Football. Tennis. Golf. Olympic shot-putting. We were just getting started. I eventually drank about eight little bottles of Chivas and passed out. When I awoke we were in Rome and he was still talking.

How to Get It: You've been at it since you were a kid. At night, you looked up at the stars and wished you were Bob Costas. You read and watched and studied and remembered, and eventually somebody came along at some rinky-dink broadcasting operation and was willing to give you money to never shut up. And you haven't.

The Upside: Like Babe Ruth, you're thrilled that somebody wants to pay you to play the game you love.

The Downside: You're not sexually attractive to straight women.

The Dark Side: You are, however, sexually attractive to straight men.

Where You Go from Here: Wherever they put idiot savants these days.

90

Talking Head/Pundit

Occupy a seat at any available table

> The one function that TV news performs very well is that when there is no news we give it to you with the same emphasis as if there were.
>
> **David Brinkley**

$$: $125,000 for your punditry, which is usually a line extension of your other pontification ventures.

ß: 80–135.

Skills Required: Be willing to go anywhere and say anything just to get your shiny head on camera.

Duties: Shed heat but no light.

Famous Example(s): Robert Novak, stooge of whatever forces inside the Administration leaked the identity of a CIA agent to him, which he published. He then had to answer questions on the issue. Pundits don't like to answer questions. So one day, on his own CNN program, *Inside Politics,* with fellow pundits Ed Henry and James Carville, he responded to some goading from Carville by exploding, saying "this is bullshit and I don't like it," and storming off in a huff. It was perhaps the least-bullshit moment in his long and boring career. Ironically, it got him fired.

> My only regret with Timothy McVeigh is he did not go to *The New York Times* building.
>
> **Ann Coulter**

How to Get It: First, you must establish some bona fides in politics, journalism, the military, whatever. Once you have, tell a television agent that you are ready to be fed into the voracious maw of the media. There are an amazing number of venues that need to be provided continual doses of strong, snazzy opinion.

The Upside: A little knowledge goes a long way.

The Downside: Having to see yourself on television is not always pleasant, because you're not very attractive.

The Dark Side: Having to get up at 5 a.m. to do a five-minute pop on *Fox and Friends.*

Where You Go from Here: The Heritage Institute.

91

The Guy Who Says Your Car Will Be Ready by Noon

We'll fix the thing eventually. I mean, we're waiting for a part. Definitely tomorrow, you know. By, like, lunchtime. Or right after.

$$: About $35 bucks an hour. A lot more, if you work on any delicate or special part of the car.

ß: 135, sliding downward when you actually have to do something next Tuesday.

> Waiting is painful. Forgetting is painful. But not knowing which to do is the worse kind of suffering.
>
> **Paulo Coelho**

Skills Required: Must know how to chew on match.

Duties: Make excuses, drink coffee, project aura of menace when need be.

Famous Examples: Larry, Fred, and Mort at the Ford dealership right across the bridge.

How to Get It: Must know how to change oil, work on car engine, look good in coveralls. Lots of guys can do that. The real gift here is the man who can hold on to a customer's car for no particular reason for days, sometimes a week longer than it was originally promised. If you've got this kind of talent for customer relations, don't hide your light under a bushel. Make sure to display it for the guy who runs the car agency. I assure you, he'll appreciate it.

The Upside: Like a business executive at the top of the corporate food chain, your entire agenda revolves around lunch (except yours is in a brown bag). Everything you do is either before lunch (in the case of stuff that should have been done the night before) or after lunch (when it should have been done in the morning).

The Downside: Customers never return, the dealership closes, you are thrown out of work, you decline into alcoholism and incontinence.

The Dark Side: You have to fix the car eventually.

Where You Go from Here: Person on the phone at your HMO who is supposed to schedule your appointment if you're sick, and puts you on hold until you hang up (see HMO Health Care Professional).

92

University Administrator

Exploit graduate students

$$: Up to $500,000 per year, if you are the president of the university that is exploiting its graduate students.

ß: 165—a base of 100, with 65 points for exploiting graduate students.

Skills Required: Shuffle paper. Hold staff meetings. Make rationalizations.

Duties: Hire teachers. Throw cocktail parties. Raise money from the alumni. Exploit graduate students.

> Our struggle is very basic. Like many workers in America today, we work for relatively low pay for a large, wealthy employer. And like many workers, we have sought to improve our working conditions through a union, to find that our employer will go to great lengths to deny its workers a real voice on the job.
>
> **Maggie Clinton, graduate student and teacher in the history department of New York University**

Famous Examples: None. These are faceless bureaucrats we're talking about. They actually have degrees in that.

How to Get It: Universities, like any large corporation, select out the least likeable, sympathetic, and selfless people to become their senior managers. Such people are adept at creating reasons why it's okay to pay somebody $10,000 per year to teach courses to hundreds of undergraduates who are paying $40,000 per year each to attend the university.

The Upside: You always feel very good about what you're doing.

The Downside: Your kid is about to enter graduate school and has started to look at you even funnier than usual.

The Dark Side: Universities still don't give their executives private jets.

Where You Go from Here: Antilabor law firm. They have Gulfstreams!

93

Velvet Rope Nazi

Establish and maintain elite fascist cadres

$$: $1,000 per night and all the blow you can stuff up your sinuses.

ß: 100, sliding down to 23. Sometimes you have to bounce people.

> I do not know who you are. I am French, I don't watch MTV. You need to take off your stupid sunglasses.
>
> **Waikiki Wally's manager to Ashley Olsen, 2005**

Skills Required: Big muscles. Strong backbone. Willingness to follow orders. Contempt for people who don't belong in the club.

Duties: Must stare down people outraged at being denied entrance, remaining cool while they scream, "Do you know who I am?!"

Famous Examples: The doorman Marc Benecke at Studio 54 in New York City, circa 1978, who according to one historian of the period, was instructed by owner/sybarite Steve Rubell to "mix a perfect salad every night," creating a situation where even celebrities were turned away at the door. "Steve once didn't like the shirt a guy was wearing," remembers Paolo Miranda, who worked there. "He told the guy he wouldn't get in with that shirt on, the guy asked if he could get in if he took it off. Steve said yes and the guy took it off and was allowed to enter the club, bare-chested. So it was really just a question of matching what Steve was looking for to add to their salad."

How to Get It: Hang around club owner, making sure to be helpful at whatever job you are asked to do, but never really achieving any definition of your duties. One day the great moment will come, and the boss says, "Hey, you. Stand at the door and make sure nobody comes in who doesn't add to the salad."

The Upside: Everybody loves you.

The Downside: Everybody hates you.

The Dark Side: The club closes. The party moves on. You are older. And one day some big stud with huge pecs tells you that you don't belong in the salad.

Where You Go from Here: Guy at the front desk, coolest restaurant in town. Let's see how Mr. Zuckerman likes being seated near the kitchen!

94

Vice President of the United States

Be prepared

> I love California. I practically grew up in Phoenix.
>
> **Dan Quayle**

$$: $198,000. Which pales, you know, beside what the job is worth afterward, when you rejoin the gigantic multinational firm you've been steering business to for the last eight years.

ß: 168—down to 0 if anything happens to the guy in the Oval Office.

Skills Required: Be very, very quiet; anything you do get involved in should not detract from the activities of the chief executive. When the president is not inclined to take the lead on something, you may be called upon to do so, so it would also be helpful not to put your foot directly into your mouth every time you open it.

Duties: Well, before the current administration, you'd have to say virtually none. Now, who knows?

> Democracy means that anyone can grow up to be president, and anyone who doesn't grow up can be vice president.
>
> **Johnny Carson**

Famous Examples: Those who went on to lead the nation, including John Adams, Thomas Jefferson, Martin Van Buren, John Tyler, Teddy Roosevelt, Harry Truman, Lyndon Johnson, Richard Nixon, and Gerald Ford, all of whose subsequent careers did much to erase the ignominy of having been vice president. Except for that, Dick Cheney.

How to Get It: Be successful enough to rate a national office, but not high enough on the political food chain to threaten the top dog on his way to the biggest supper bowl on the planet.

The Upside: Great title, decent perks, very little job responsibility (except for Dick Cheney).

The Downside: Everybody makes fun of the office and thinks it's completely superfluous (except for Dick Cheney).

The Dark Side: You da man. What have you got to show for it? (Except for Dick Cheney).

Where You Go from Here: Back to Halliburton.

95

Wine Industry Professional

Make extremely portentous and serious that which is essentially frivolous and arbitrary

> Before forty eating is beneficial. After forty, drinking.
>
> **The Talmud**

$$: Very low, if you have to touch grapes. Very high, if all you do is sniff at things.

ß: 191, except for the wine itself, which is very nice.

Skills Required: Study. Work hard. Train your palate as if it were a dancing dog. Learn to talk the talk. And drink! Drink!

Duties: From the wine riddler who turns the bottles in their cradles, to the wine pourer who allows credulous monkeys to taste little dollops prior to their purchase, to the sommelier who makes diners feel inadequate to the task of selecting their drinks, to the critic who compares the slight hint of chocolate to the subtle undertow of citrus and nutmeg, the field of wine is full of grapes.

Famous Examples: As far as I'm concerned, we're all just a couple of bottles away from the stinky guy in the greasy raincoat standing on the corner with a bottle of muscatel in a brown paper bag.

> **Jack:** If they want to drink merlot, we're drinking merlot.
>
> **Miles:** No, if anyone orders merlot, I'm leaving. I am *not* drinking any fucking merlot!
>
> **Jack:** If they want to drink merlot, we're drinking merlot.
>
> **Miles:** No, if anyone orders merlot, I'm leaving. I am *not* drinking any fucking merlot!
>
> **Alexander Payne, *Sideways***

How to Get It: You can be in the wine industry if you can read this without gagging: "Dark chocolate and plum fruits court a deceptive play of substantial ripe tannins and, at this relatively early stage, provide for a more powerful Grange stamp on the palate than on the nose. Oak plays a supportive role and is perfectly integrated and absorbed. This is a wine of admirable balance and poise, with trademark mid-palate richness."

The Upside: Drink all the time and see yourself as a connoisseur, not a stumblebum.

The Downside: You snore sitting up in a chair with your eyes open.

The Dark Side: Your liver is the size of a pumpkin.

Where You Go from Here: Into your basement, never to return.

96

Writer of This Book

Work way too hard for too little money

> May the Schwartz be with you.
>
> **Mel Brooks, *Spaceballs***

$$: Looks good in the beginning, but after the project turns out to be far more demanding than you ever contemplated, seems insufficient.

ß: 14. Writing about bullshit is serious work.

Skills Required: Must be able to maintain concentration day after day, be amusing even when you're in a bad mood for a variety of reasons that are not anybody's business, meet deadlines only you consider insane.

Duties: Write funny, trenchant, enormously popular book without popping aneurysm.

Famous Example(s): Hello.

How to Get It: Meet with editors over lunch. Cook up idea so that lunch is not a total waste. Call agent, tell her that it looks like fun, not too hard, blah blah blah. Seal deal. Take first portion of advance. Spend it. Wait until book is almost due. Wait longer. Write book on BlackBerry. Hand in book. Be tortured by editors over a variety of minor bullshit; no more nice lunches, just bad sandwiches and warm soda. Receive second portion of advance. Send to ex-wife. Wait for publication of book. Book is published! Hopefully, you are reading this while standing up in an airport bookstore. Buy it!

The Upside: Do *Charlie Rose.* Win valuable prizes.

The Downside: Give up morning nap to write on train rides.

The Dark Side: Risk drowning in your own bullshit.

Where You Go from Here: Available upon request.

Xerox Repairman

Fix things so that they remain broken

$$: $39,500. You make a lot more in overtime, so it helps to make sure things break again near closing time.

> If it's broke, don't fix it.
>
> **Xerox philosophy**

ß: 3. Having your friggin' Xerox down is no joke.

Skills Required: Willingness to move continually between the several predetermined places day after day.

Duties: Come to office in need of immediate repair of copying machine. Stare at machine. Stoop down. Open machine. Tinker. Effect adjustments that last exactly as long as it takes your elevator to reach the ground floor.

Famous Example: Fred.

How to Get It: I don't know. And if I did, I wouldn't tell you.

The Upside: Lots of fresh air and sunshine.

The Downside: Everybody yakking at you all the time about blown deadlines and shit.

The Dark Side: Trapped in a very small room with four or five angry middle managers.

Where You Go from Here: Maintenance, nuclear power plant.

98

Yeti

Be strong, silent, and mysteriously unavailable

$$: Unknown.

ß: Complete.

Skills Required: Stay out of sight. Have big feet.

Duties: Dart into view after ascertaining that nobody around has a decent camera. After that, you're on your own.

Famous Examples: The original yeti may be found, or not found, in Tibet, which itself is not that easy to find. The word "yeti" means "magical creature" in Tibetan. Those who have almost seen it believe it is something like a man and also like a huge ape, very hairy. Like any elusive celebrity,

> Unquestionably, the figure in outline was exactly like a human being, walking upright and stopping occasionally to uproot or pull at some dwarf rhododendron bushes. It showed up dark against the snow and, as far as I could make out, wore no clothes.
>
> **N. A. Tombazi, Greek photographer, 1925**

the yeti is also the center of a huge industry related to its nonactivities and absence of presence. Other examples: Bigfoot, a denizen of the northwestern United States; Tim Robbins and Susan Sarandon, except when they have a movie out.

> I want to be left alone.
>
> **Greta Garbo**

How to Get It: Just get out of Dodge. If you see paparazzi looking for you, leave nothing but footprints.

The Upside: Nobody bothers you, ever.

The Downside: Kind of cold out there.

The Dark Side: When somebody finds out you're the yeti they've heard so much about, their whole attitude toward you changes entirely.

Where You Go from Here: Scotland.

99

Yoga Franchiser

Copyright and market wisdom of the ages

> Because I have balls like atom bombs, two of them, 100 megatons each. Nobody fucks with me.
>
> **Bikram Choudhury, Yoga franchiser, explaining why he has the right to copyright a 5,000-year-old form of meditation and exercise**

$$: From enough to pay for your brown rice to millions and millions, if you're a predatory, litigious yogi out to protect your piece of this $25 billion business.

ß: Get bent.

Skills Required: Transform the selfless, timeless wisdom of the East into disgusting greed.

Duties: Sue small yoga instructors for control of the ancient positions.

Famous Example(s): Bikram Choudhury, the founder of the worldwide Yoga College of India, which is also trademarked. He was born in Calcutta in 1946, and began yoga at the age of four. At the age of thirteen, he won the National India Yoga Championship. As a young man, Bikram was asked by his yogi to start schools in India. These were so successful that he then moved on to Japan, and then to the United States, where there are now more than 900 franchisees providing Bikram Yoga.

> Any attempt by an individual to own a Yoga style runs counter to the general spirit of Yoga and degrades the energy created by its teachers and practitioners . . . and is outrageous, disreputable and arguably contrary to the copyright laws of the United States.
>
> **Open Source Yoga Unity, an organization representing mom-and-pop yoga studios**

How to Get It: Somewhere along the line, Bikram reduced yoga to twenty-six formal postures, to be done in a certain order, often in a sadistically hot room. He then trademarked his method and franchised it out to all those who wanted to run Bikram Yoga studios. That's one thing. More recently, however, he has contended that anybody teaching the practice of yoga is, in fact, encroaching on his trademark. He has been quite successful in scaring a bunch of mom-and-pop operations out of business, until these generally peaceful and nonconfrontational folk have gotten together and formed Open Source Yoga Unity (OSYU), which has gone to court to protect the freedom to practice yoga that is not trademarked. Bikram has a lot more money than they do, though.

The Upside: Really fun to kick people's asses—with yoga!

The Downside: There are still some jerks out there doing yoga who aren't paying you for the right to do it.

The Dark Side: People who never hated anybody now hate you.

Where You Go from Here: Trademark trees, so nobody can sit under them without paying you a small stipend.

You

Whatever it is YOU do

> You are so beautiful to me. . . .
>
> **Joe Cocker**

$$: Not as great as you'd like quite yet, but you're gonna do better!

ß: None. Or a ton. It's up to you.

Skills Required: Whatever you got, baby.

Duties: You can work hard or hardly work.

Famous Example: You, pal!

How to Get It: Be yourself. And when you need to skate a little faster because the ice is thin, just lace 'em up and do it!

The Upside: You've got no place to go but up!

The Downside: Hard to imagine! Why would there be any downside?

The Dark Side: Sometimes you have to sleep, so you can't be with yourself 24/7!

Where You Go from Here: Anyplace you like, my friend. And may the road rise up to meet you as you go!

Conclusion

Transforming your job into a bullshit job

Just a word before we say good-bye.

It may be that as you go through this vale of tears we call our working life, you will never be fortunate enough to acquire one of the truly satisfying and lucrative bullshit jobs profiled in this humble effort.

Don't be down. While there are many occupations that immediately convey upon their owners a full measure of bullshit, it is equally true that, with pluck, luck, and perseverance, virtually every job can be transformed into one with a good, healthy portion of the stuff.

The key lies in three important principles:

1. Delegation
2. Procrastination
3. Abnegation

"Delegation" is a polite term for asking other people to do the things that you, by all rights, should be doing. It is practiced by all those who call management their home.

"Procrastination" means never doing today what you could possibly do tomorrow, or even next week. Masters of the art control their time better than those who are beholden to more superficially realistic schedules.

And abnegation? That is the moment when we say, aw, the hell with it, and bag the task completely. It's amazing how many things not done turn out to have been not worth doing.

In the end, a life that is made up of nothing but bullshit is as untenable as one that is completely dedicated to content. It is your gift on this earth, your right as a living, sentient human being, to fight for the right mix.

In that balance lies fulfillment, peace, and even a little happiness.